THE POST-WAR WORLD

THE USA
SINCE 1945

ELIZABETH CAMPLING

B.T. Batsford Ltd, London

CONTENTS

First published 1988

Typeset by Tek-Art Ltd, Kent
and printed in Great Britain
by Anchor Brendon
Tiptree, Essex
for the publishers
B.T. Batsford Ltd
4, Fitzhardinge Street
London W1H 0AH

ISBN 0 7134 5756 2

Acknowledgments
The Author and Publishers would like to thank the following for permission to reproduce illustrations: Associated Press for pages 30, 46, 56, 58; AP/Wide World Photos for pages 28, 30, 41; The BBC Hulton Picture Library for the frontispiece and pages 8, 11, 12, 18, 19, 22, 23, 39, 44, 48, 54; NASA for page 32; The Keystone Press Agency for pages 6, 14, 15(b), 26(a), 34, 37, 38, 42, 47, 50, 51; The Photo Source Ltd for pages 15(a), 26(b).

Cover illustrations
(*Top*) Martin Luther King (courtesy Paul Popper Ltd); (*bottom left*) Ronald Reagan compaigning in the 1980 Presidential elections (courtesy The Press Association); (*bottom centre*) Anti-War demonstration at Lincoln Memorial, 1967 (courtesy Paul Popper Ltd); (*bottom right*) Neil Armstrong, first astronaut on the moon (courtesy NASA).

The frontispiece shows the Capitol building, seat of Congress in Washington DC.

1 THE USA IN 1945

Roosevelt had been re-elected in 1936, 1940 and 1944.

1945 saw the United States on the threshold of a new era. On 12 April Franklin D. Roosevelt, a Democrat who had been President since 1932, died and was replaced by Vice-President Harry S. Truman, who was little known to the public and inexperienced in international affairs. He told newspapermen that evening, 'I feel as though the moon and all the stars and planets have fallen on me'.

The Second World War was drawing to a close, Germany surrendering on 8 May and Japan on 2 September. With Europe in ruins, the United States and the Soviet Union now stood alone as the world's two most powerful nations – the Superpowers. The United States also possessed a lethal new weapon, the atomic bomb, which the Russians did not. To the inexperienced President would fall the task of guiding the many difficult decisions that would have to be made about the role the United States was to play in the post-war world and also about the future shape of American society itself.

The correct names for the two nations are the 'United States of America' and the 'Soviet Union', not 'America' (which is a continent and includes Latin America and Canada) or 'Russia' (which is only one part of the Soviet Union.) As the two terms are so often used inter-changeably, however, both will be used in this book.

The government of the United States

The American system of government is a democratic and federal one. Each state is responsible for its own internal affairs, while the federal government in Washington D.C. deals with the big issues of war, peace, defence and the overall direction of the economy.

There were 48 states in 1945; 50 – after the addition of Alaska and Hawaii in 1959.

Within the federal government, the President shares power with Congress, which has to approve all laws and most large expenditures. This system was designed deliberately by the Founding Fathers in 1787 so that Congress could provide a check against any President becoming too powerful or too corrupt. It was known as the 'separation of powers'. A third branch of the federal government, the Supreme Court, keeps a check on all the others through its ability to declare that laws passed by Congress or the practices of individual states are 'unconstitutional'.

Founding Fathers is the popular name given to the men like George Washington, John Adams and Thomas Jefferson, who led the break with England in the War of Independence and drew up the Constitution in 1787.

The President is elected every four years by popular vote, but part of each House of Congress – the Senate and the House of Representatives – stands for re-election every two years (mid-term elections). Thus it is possible for a President to be faced in the middle of his term of office with a Congress dominated by the opposition party.

In addition to his democratic right to vote governments in and out of office, the rights of the individual citizen are supposedly protected against a misuse of government power by the Bill of Rights. These rights, which cannot easily be taken away, include freedom of speech, religion and the press, the right to trial by jury, the right of peaceful assembly and the right to bear arms for self-protection.

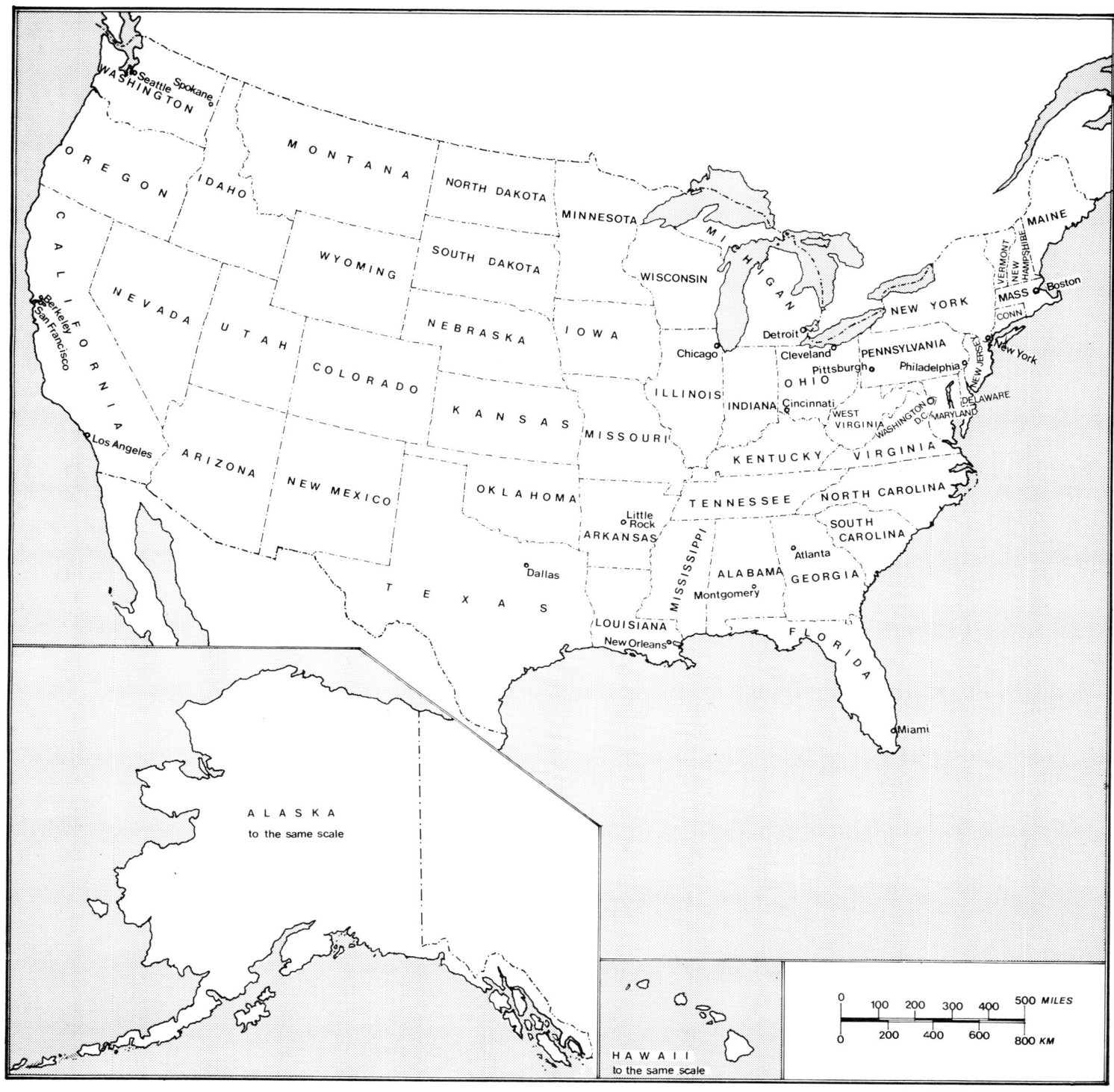

Map of the USA, showing the major cities and states.

The Dixiecrats were from the old Confederate states of North and South Carolina, Georgia, Alabama, Mississippi, Louisiana, Virginia, Texas, Arkansas and Florida.

In 1945 there were two major political parties, the Republicans and Democrats, both of which represented a wide spectrum of opinion. Republicans tended to support big business and the right of states to run their own affairs without interference from Washington ('states' rights'), Democrats to be more concerned with the underprivileged and more tolerant of Federal interference. This distinction should not be taken too far, however. In 1945 there were 'liberal' Republicans, and the southern wing of the Democratic Party – the Dixiecrats – was markedly racist and jealously guarded the states' rights of the Southern states.

The atom bomb

The war in Europe was almost over by the time Truman became President but the Japanese were proving more difficult to beat. The battles for Iwo Jima (17 February-17 March) and Okinawa (1 April-21 June), two of the outlying islands of the Japanese archipelago, cost the lives of 61,000 Americans and over 100,000 Japanese soldiers and civilians. In July the Japanese Government rejected surrender terms, and in the same month an atom bomb was successfully tested in New Mexico.

Inside the American government, opinion was divided over what should be done next. Some argued that an invasion of mainland Japan would cost so many lives on both sides that they would be justified in using the bomb to frighten Japan into a rapid surrender. Others argued against this, both on moral grounds and from the fear that it would trigger off a worldwide nuclear arms race that would endanger the United States herself. The Franck Committee, a group of Chicago scientists who had worked on preparing plutonium for the bomb, petitioned the President in June:

All of us familiar with the present state of nucleonics [nuclear science] live with the vision before our eyes of sudden destruction visited on our own country, of a Pearl Harbour disaster repeated in one thousand times magnification in every one of our major cities.

In the end, Stimson's view prevailed, and an atomic bomb was dropped on the city of Hiroshima on 6 August 1945, killing about 100,000 civilians immediately, fatally injuring a further 100,000 through heat and radiation and flattening the city. On 9 August a second bomb was dropped, this time on Nagasaki, killing 50,000. Japan surrendered on 2 September.

The case for using the bomb was argued most persuasively by the Secretary of War, Henry Stimson. In a memorandum sent to President Truman on 2 July 1945 he stressed that the conquest of Japan by land would take until the end of 1946 and cost over one million American and several million Japanese casualties.

From the Franck Committee *Report on the Social and Political Implications of the Atomic Bomb*, 12 June 1946.

On 7 December 1941 Japanese planes bombed the US fleet at Pearl Harbor on Hawaii.

Robert Oppenheimer, head of the atomic bomb project, and General Groves surveying the site of the first successful atomic bomb test in New Mexico in July 1945. The steel tower that held the bomb has been melted by the heat of the explosion and the surrounding land burnt into glass-like cinders. The fact that the two men are standing there without protection shows how little was understood at the time about the dangers of radiation.

The origins of the Cold War

By 1945 most Americans shared Roosevelt's belief that 'great power brings great responsibility' – and there was little chance that the United States would return to the isolationism of the 1930s. Victory had bred confidence in the superiority of the 'American way of life' and an urge to spread the benefits of democracy and free-enterprise worldwide.

By April 1945 this vision of the post-war world seemed under threat from the Soviet Union, America's ally in the war against Germany. Although Stalin (Communist Party Secretary and Soviet leader) had promised Roosevelt that the Eastern European nations liberated by the Red Army in 1944 and 1945 would be allowed to decide their futures by democratic election, puppet Communist governments were already being installed in Poland, Rumania and Bulgaria, and Truman no longer trusted that Stalin would keep his word. When the two met at the Potsdam Conference in July, the atmosphere was fraught with mutual suspicion.

No one was yet sure, however, just how far the Russians intended to go, and the United States was anyway unprepared for conflict with a nation that had until only recently been an ally. For two long years a cautious policy of waiting and watching was adopted, while Americans debated the nature of the Soviet threat and what should be done about it.

Some, like George Kennan, an official in the American embassy in Moscow, argued that Russia was bent on world conquest, and unless she were stopped would 'flow into every nook and cranny available to it in the basin of the world'. Henry Wallace, Truman's Secretary of Commerce, disagreed. Having been invaded so many times in the past and having lost 20 million of her citizens in the last war, Russia was naturally preoccupied with her security, and her behaviour in Eastern Europe was rooted in fear rather than in aggression. In that case:

> . . . the action to improve the situation is clearly indicated. The fundamental objective of such action should be to allay any reasonable fear, suspicion and distrust . . . . We should be prepared, even at the expense of risking epithets of apeasement, to agree to reasonable Russian guarantees of security.

Isolationism: the refusal of the USA in the 1930s to become involved in the affairs of Europe, regarding them as irrelevant to the country's vital national interests.

During these two years a Communist government was installed in Hungary and co-operation in ruling Germany was also breaking down.

Kennan's telegram, sent to Washington from Moscow in February 1946, is one of the key documents of post-1945 American foreign policy.

Wallace in a confidential letter to Truman on 23 July 1946. When Wallace made the dispute public Truman sacked him.

Truman (centre) with Stalin (second left) and Churchill at the Potsdam Conference in July 1945. The surface cordiality hid an atmosphere fraught with distrust, that was to develop in the Cold War.

If, argued Wallace, the United States failed to understand that Russia was more interested in having friendly than democratic governments in Eastern Europe and reacted only with hostile suspicion, relations between the Superpowers would continue to deteriorate.

The American way of life

Throughout their history Americans had prided themselves on their 'rugged individualism'. It was the duty of a man to look after himself and his dependants and not rely on the government for help. By implication, those who could not manage had no one but themselves to blame. The way to a prosperous society lay in harnessing this individualism. Most men would work harder for themselves than for other people and the wealth that was thus created would 'trickle down' through the economy to the eventual benefit of all. This was the basis of the 'free enterprise', or 'capitalist' economy.

In an attempt to overcome the widespread suffering of the Great Depression of the 1930s, President Roosevelt introduced a new idea into American politics. Only the federal government, he argued, not individuals, had the power and resources to alleviate the effects of the Depression. His programme, the New Deal, set up job-creation schemes, provided limited welfare payments and passed legislation to protect the rights of the labour (trade) unions. Federal schemes like the Tennessee Valley Authority (TVA) overrode states' rights. Supporters of the New Deal, who were mostly from the Democratic Party, were called 'liberals'. Most Republicans disapproved and labelled it 'creeping communism'.

The New Deal's assumption that the government was ultimately responsible for the welfare of its citizens was revolutionary but designed to cope only with a specific emergency, not with chronic poverty or with the disasters that hit individuals in normal times. Roosevelt himself often said that it would be phased out once the economy was operating normally again. In 1945 it remained to be seen whether the cult of 'rugged individualism' would come back into fashion now that the Depression was over, or whether liberal principles would be extended to cope with America's long-term social problems.

Civil rights

Although slavery had been abolished in the United States in the 1860s, Blacks had continued to be treated as second-class citizens and to be denied their civil rights. The Southern states practised segregation – the provision of separate and unequal facilities for Blacks and Whites, similar to Apartheid in South Africa – and by a combination of legal tricks and intimidation also denied Blacks their right to vote. In the North, where over 50 per cent of Blacks lived by 1950, there was no legal apparatus of segregation but much unofficial discrimination in housing and employment. Most Blacks were caught up in a 'cycle of deprivation'. It was difficult for them to get any jobs but the most menial, and low pay forced them to live in the poorest areas of town. As Blacks moved in, all the Whites who could moved out, turning whole areas of inner cities into black ghettos, like Harlem (New York) or Watts (Los Angeles). Local schools were poor, and black children tended to leave early, qualified only for the unskilled jobs their fathers had had. Thus poverty and hopelessness were passed on from generation to generation. Only a few extraordinarily talented or determined Blacks managed to break out of the cycle.

Presidents ignored the problem as far as possible. Race relations were the responsibility of the individual states, and any President who overrode states'

The Great Depression had begun with the Wall Street crash of October 1929. At its height in 1932-3, 15 million Americans (a quarter of the workforce) were unemployed and there was no safety net of social security.

The TVA was a scheme to prevent annual flooding and to harness the waters of the Tennessee River, which ran through seven states, for agriculture and hydro-electric power.

It was estimated that even in good times one-fifth of the American population lived below the poverty line.

One stratagem was the literacy test as evidence that a person was educated enough to vote intelligently. It was up to the local registrar, who was invariably white, to decide who passed and who did not. Registrars regularly failed Blacks for no good reason, while automatically passing Whites, no matter how illiterate they might be.

The best examples of Blacks who broke through the cycle are to be found in the worlds of sport and entertainment, such as the jazz musicians Louis Armstrong and Duke Ellington, the athlete Jesse Owens (who won gold medals at the 1938 Berlin Olympics) and the boxer Cassius Clay (later Muhammad Ali).

A gathering of the Ku Klux Klan in the South. The Klan existed to keep Blacks in a position of fear and inferiority.

Throughout the war the US army remained segregated and Blacks were not allowed to become officers. The navy, however, was gradually desegregated.

From an article in September 1944 by Grant Reynolds, who spent nearly three years as a chaplin on active duty with the US army.

rights in this matter would lose millions of white votes in the South. This particularly affected the Democrats, who traditionally drew much support from that area.

For decades, Blacks had appeared to accept their second-class status with resignation. During the war, however, they had faced the same dangers and hardships as Whites and had been told continually that they were fighting to protect democracy and freedom. Among black servicemen, at least, a new mood had begun to surface by 1945:

But he [the black soldier] also knows that there is a lot of unfinished business about human decency that he would like to see cleared up before he becomes a corpse for any country. To deny him food when he is hungry, dignified transport when he has to travel, a voice in choosing those who rule him . . . and then propagandize him daily into becoming a hero for democracy is nauseating to say the least.

Conclusion

By the end of 1945 the United States stood on the verge of two great crises. A new mood of self-assertiveness among Blacks made it likely that the long-buried civil rights issue would soon come to a head. The survival of racial prejuduce among many white Americans made it equally likely that the crisis would be prolonged and perhaps even violent.

Relations with the Soviet Union were rapidly deteriorating. Much of the future of the United States and the whole post-war world would depend on whether the Truman government decided to oppose or appease Russia. The Kennan/Wallace debate of 1946-7 is echoed by historians today, who are still arguing over which Superpower was most to blame for the Cold War.

Most ominous of all was the problem of the atom bomb. With each passing month it seemed more and more likely that the Franck Committee's conclusions were correct. In the short term, using the bomb to defeat Japan had been a spectacular success. In the long term, it opened the way to a new and more deadly arms race.

2 CONTAINMENT AND ITS CRITICS: AMERICAN FOREIGN POLICY 1945-60

American presidential elections take place in November every four years, but the new President is not inaugurated (takes up office) until January of the following year. The correct dates for Eisenhower's first term are, therefore, 1953-7. It is much more common, however, to date Presidents from election to election, and that is the method used in this book.

The first successful Soviet atomic test was in 1949.

Greek Civil War 1945-9 between the forces of King Paul, restored by the British in 1945, and communist guerillas, aided by Yugoslavia but not openly by Russia.

Source A
From the speech by President Truman to a joint session of Congress, 12 March 1947.

Presidents:
Harry S. Truman 1945-52
Dwight D. Eisenhower ('Ike') 1952-60

By 1947 the Truman administration was convinced that the Soviet Union was set on spreading communism worldwide but was not sure just how the United States could stop this process. Monopoly of the atomic bomb up to 1949 brought few advantages, for after the horrors of Hiroshima there was great reluctance even to think of using it again. And no one was quite sure how close the Soviet Union was to developing nuclear weapons of her own and being able to retaliate in kind. It was in the face of this dilemma that the policy of containment, which was to dominate American thinking for the next 20 years, was born.

The Truman Doctrine

The moment of decision came in February 1947 when Britain announced that she could no longer afford to send aid to the non-Communists in the Greek civil war. Truman went up to Capitol Hill (where Congress meets) in person and asked Congress for a $400 million grant for the Greek anti-Communists. In his accompanying speech he set out what became known as the Truman Doctrine or the policy of Containment. Congress granted the money.

At the present moment in world history nearly every nation must choose between alternative ways of life. The choice is too often not a free one.

One way of life is based on the will of the majority, and is distinguished by free institutions, representative government, free elections, guarantees of individual liberty, freedom of speech and religion and freedom from political oppression.

The second way of life is based on the will of a minority forcibly imposed on the majority. It relies upon terror and oppression, a controlled press and radio, fixed elections, and the suppression of personal freedoms.

I believe that it must be the policy of the United States to support free peoples who are resisting attempted subjugation by armed minorities or by outside pressures.

I believe that we must assist free peoples to work out their own destinies in their own way.

I believe that our help should be primarily through economic and financial aid . . . for the seeds of totalitarian regimes are nutured by misery and want.

Source B
From a series of articles by Walter Lippmann, journalist and political commentator, in *The New York Herald Tribune*, 1947.

Heterogeneous: mixed, having little in common.

The policy of Containment . . . demands the employment of American economic, political, and in the last analysis, American military power at sectors in the interior of Europe and Asia. This requires, as I have pointed out, ground forces which we do not possess.

The policy can be implemented only by recruiting, subsidizing and supporting a heterogeneous army of satellites, clients, dependants and puppets . . . . We must stake our own security and the peace of the world upon satellites . . . about whom we know very little. Frequently they will act for their own reasons or on their own judgements, presenting us with accomplished facts that we did not intend, and crises for which we are unready . . . . We shall either have to disown our puppets, which would be tantamount to defeat and loss of face, or must support them at an incalculable cost on an unintended, unforeseen and perhaps undesirable issue.

? ?

1 What two rival political systems does Truman refer to in Source A? What side should the United States take in the struggle between them?

2 To what kind of help does Truman commit the USA? What unspoken limits does he place on US aid and why does he impose them?

3 Lippmann sympathizes with Truman's aims but thinks the commitment unwise. On what grounds does he base his doubts? As you read the rest of this book, think about the extent to which Lippmann's fears have been justified between 1947 and the 1980s.

Marshall Aid and the future of Europe

Truman's plan to stop the spread of communism by economic and political means soon had its first success. The economies of Western Europe were slow to recover from the ravages of war and there was a very real chance that elections would bring Communists to power in France and Italy, fulfilling Truman's prediction that 'the seeds of totalitarian regimes are nutured by misery and want'. In May 1947 Secretary of State (Foreign Minister) George Marshall offered all the nations of Europe, including the Soviet Union, an outright gift of $12.5 billion to rebuild their economies. While Russia refused on behalf of herself and her satellites, the Marshall Plan enabled the economies of Western Europe to stage a spectacular recovery, and the danger of communism there receded.

Czechoslovakia, which had been governed since 1945 by a coalition in which both Communists and non-Communists took part, tried to accept Marshall Aid. Fearful that she might slip into the Western camp, pro-Soviet Communists took the country over completely in February 1948. This served to deepen Western suspicions of Soviet intentions.

The Truman Doctrine committed the US to the defence of Western Europe. The years 1948 and 1949 saw the Berlin Airlift (the joint efforts by the American and allied air forces to supply West Berlin by air during the Soviet blocade of the city between June 1948 and May 1949), the creation of a state of West Germany (Federal Republic of Germany) out of the British, French and American zones of occupation, and the foundation of NATO (North Atlantic Treaty Organization), a mutual defence pact between the USA, Canada and ten European nations.

The Soviet Union retaliated by forming her zone into the state of East Germany (German Democratic Republic) in 1949.

The now-entrenched rivalry between the Superpowers became known as the 'Cold War' and was 'fought' within limits that both sides respected and which were to remain unchanged for the next 20 years: On the American side the spread of communism was to be resisted but there was to be no attempt to win back countries already in the Soviet bloc by 1947, for such a threat to Soviet security might provoke a third world war. Both sides were careful to stop short of a face-to-face confrontation, even if this entailed a humiliating climb-down. During the Berlin blockade, for example, the Russians made no serious attempt to shoot down blockade-running planes, and Truman rejected military advice to break the blockade by force.

Funds from Marshall Aid being used to rebuild damaged houses in West Berlin. The notice reads: 'Berlin is rebuilding with the help of Marshall Aid.'

The Korean War

The strengths and weaknesses of the Containment policy were tested in the Korean War (1950-3). In June 1950 communist North Korea invaded the non-Communist South. Under the flag of the United Nations, an army, composed mainly of American troops, commanded by General Douglas MacArthur, was sent to the defence of South Korea. Landing behind North Korean lines at Inchon, MacArthur took his opponents by surprise. In under a month the South was cleared of North Korean troops and the original aim fulfilled. With Truman's permission, MacArthur now overstepped the limits of containment and invaded North Korea itself in the hope of rooting out communism there. By November the country had been overrun and the UN army had reached the border with China at the Yalu River. At this point the Chinese intervened, and MacArthur was forced to retreat back to the 38th Parallel.

During the retreat an argument broke out between the President and the General. In order to hold on to North Korea, MacArthur urged that factories and supply lines inside China herself be bombed, and even suggested that the ousted Nationalist leader, Jiang Jieshi, be encouraged to exploit this opportunity to invade and regain the mainland. Truman argued that the Chinese had probably only intervened out of fear for their own security and were no threat to South Korea, whose defence had been the original UN objective. MacArthur refused to accept this verdict and made his disagreement public.

In 1945 Korea had been divided along the 38th line of latitude as a temporary measure, similar to that in Germany. As no agreement could be reached on terms for reunification, the two Superpowers each set up a model state in her own half and withdrew in 1948. The US was able to get Security Council approval for the invasion because the Russians were boycotting the Council in protest against US refusal to let the People's Republic of China (Communist China) occupy the Chinese seat at the UN.

In 1949 Chinese Communists under Mao Zedong had defeated the Nationalist (Guomindang) government of Jiang Jieshi and established the People's Republic of China. Jiang fled to the offshore island of Taiwan (Formosa), which became the state of Nationalist China. The US continued to recognize the Nationalists as the only legitimate government of all China.

A hero's return. After his dismissal by President Truman, General McArthur arrives in San Francisco to an enthusiastic reception from the American people.

Source A
From Truman's broadcast to the nation, 11 April 1951.

In the simplest terms what we are doing in Korea is this: we are trying to prevent a third world war.

I think most people in this country recognized that fact last June . . . . Now many persons, even some who applauded our decision to defend South Korea, have forgotten the basic reason for our action . . . . The Communists in the Kremlin are engaged in a monstrous conspiracy to stamp out freedom all over the world . . . . The only question is: when is the best time to meet that threat and how?

The best time to meet the threat is in the beginning. It is easier to put out a fire in the beginning when it is small than after it has become a roaring blaze . . . .

So far, by fighting a limited war in Korea, we have prevented agression from succeeding and the ability of the whole free world to resist Communist aggression has been greatly improved.

We have taught the enemy a lesson. He has found out that aggression is not cheap or easy. We do not want to see the conflict in Korea extended. We are trying to prevent a world war – not start one, and if we do these other things [MacArthur's suggestions] we shall be running a very grave risk of starting a general war. If that were to happen, we should have brought about the very situation we were trying to prevent . . . .

A number of events have made it evident that General MacArthur did not agree with this policy. I have considered it essential to relieve General MacArthur so that there would be no doubt about the real aim and purpose of our policy.

Source B
From General MacArthur's testimony before the Senate, 19 April 1951.

While I was not consulted prior to the President's decision to intervene in support of the Republic of Korea, the decision . . . proved a sound one, as we hurled back the invader and decimated his forces . . . . Our victory was complete and our objectives within reach when Red China intervened with numerically superior forces. This created a new war and a new situation, a situation that called for new decisions. Such decisions have not been forthcoming.

? ?

1 On what occasion was Truman's speech in source A made and why did Truman consider it necessary to take this action?

2 What is the basic disagreement between Truman and MacArthur over the aims and purpose of the Korean War?

3 Why should such a difference of view have arisen and who is to blame?

4 Most of the senior generals agreed with Truman's actions, but the sacking of MacArthur was very unpopular among ordinary Americans. How can this be explained?

No final peace treaty has ever been signed and the two Koreas still refuse to accept each other's right to exist.

A new commander, General Ridgeway, was appointed, and United Nations troops did not try to invade North Korea again, nor did the Chinese attempt to invade the South. The war degenerated into a war of attrition around the 38th Parallel, in which sides attempted to wear each other down by constant skirmishes and disruption of supplies until a truce was signed in July 1953.

Eisenhower and Dulles

Eisenhower's Secretary of State was John Foster Dulles, a sternly religious man with a tendency to see world problems in black and white moral terms. During the 1952 election campaign he suggested some changes in American foreign policy.

Source A
From 'The Policy of Boldness', an article by J.F. Dulles published in *Life* magazine, 19 May 1952.

The peoples of Eastern Europe and China.

Source B
Averell Harriman, former US ambassador to the Soviet Union, in a television debate with Dulles in August 1952.

Iron curtain: the name first used in 1946 by Churchill, to describe the division between the democratic West and the Communist East.

Source C
From a *Washington Post* editorial, September 1952.

There exists a moral and natural law determining right and wrong, to which men must in the long run conform, and America is the chosen agent of God's vengeance. This law has been trampled on by the Soviet Union, and for that violation they can and should be made to pay. America must make it known that it wishes and expects liberation to occur, for that will electrify the captive peoples and heap new burdens upon their jailers.

It's very dangerous to talk about liberation because nothing can be more cruel than to get the people behind the Iron Curtain – I have been there and I know what it is – to try to revolt. You would have a new tragedy and a massacre.

The Europeans see him [Dulles] as a fire-breathing warrior who would obliterate Europe with hydrogen bombs in order to free Poland.

? ?

1 In what significant way does Dulles want to change American policy?

2 Why do Dulles' critics in sources B and C see his ideas as both dangerous and impracticable?

3 What difference in personal backgrounds and experiences might help to explain the differing world views of Dulles and his critics? Be careful to take into consideration the atmosphere inside the US at this time (see Chapter 3).

John Foster Dulles (centre) in conversation with Eisenhower (left) and Prime Minister Fanfani of Italy.

Stalin had died in 1953 and had been replaced as Party Secretary by Nikita Khrushchev.

In 1951 Iranian Prime Minister Mossadegh nationalized the Anglo-Iranian Oil Company. Seeing this as a sign of Communist influence instead of as the gesture of Iranian national pride that it really was, America backed the deposed Shah in a successful bid to regain his throne. As a reward, the USA received a 40 per cent share in Iranian oil production and the lasting suspicion of the Muslim world.

For Vietnam and Cuba, see pp. 36 and 33.

The area that most concerned America was the former French colony of Indo-China, which had been divided in 1954 in four states – Laos, Cambodia (Kampuchea), Communist North Veitnam and non-Communist South Vietnam. The USA immediately committed herself to keeping communism out of South Vietnam.

American behaviour between 1952 and 1960 reflected these contradictions. Dulles' more extreme views were watered down by Eisenhower's greater realism and common sense, and the basic strategy of Containment remained intact. On the other hand, some ominous trends in US foreign policy were strengthened. The main developments of this period were:

1 When a revolt did occur behind the Iron Curtain – in Hungary in 1956 – the United States made no attempt to intervene to prevent its brutal suppression by the Red Army.

2 Proposals for a Summit Conference between the American and Soviet leaders in 1953 and 1954 were overruled by Dulles. When one did take place, in Geneva in 1955 (see p. 16), ideas for arms control came to nothing.

3 The US became increasingly liable to view developments in other countries purely as off-shoots of the Cold War and to ignore the local issues at stake. Left-wing revolutionary movements of all kinds were seen as Soviet-inspired and, therefore, a danger to American security. A number of unpopular and undemocratic regimes were backed by the United States solely on the grounds that they were anti-Communist, recalling Lippmann's warning in 1947. Examples of this can be found in Vietnam, Iran (something the Iranians never forgot) and Cuba.

4 The Central Intelligence Agency (CIA), headed by Dulles' brother, Allen, became increasingly influential and intervened regularly in the affairs of other countries, subverting governments that it considered hostile to US interests. The CIA was answerable to no one but the President and did not have to account for its actions before Congress. It therefore provided Presidents with a way of carrying on a secret foreign policy behind the backs of Congress and the electorate.

5 American interest in South-East Asia was intensified by Eisenhower's adoption of the Domino Theory. If one South-East Asian country fell to communism, it was argued, then its neighbours would soon follow suit, just as all the dominoes in a row collapse when the first one is knocked down.

6 With the death of Stalin, East-West tensions eased somewhat. This was known as the 'thaw'. After Dulles' death in 1959, top-level visits were exchanged, Vice-President Nixon going to Moscow and Khruschev touring

Summit: a conference of the top Superpower leaders.

As the American plane was shot down over 1000 miles inside Soviet territory, Eisenhower could not deny that it had been on a spying mission. He did, however, refuse Khruschev's demand for a public apology, on the grounds that the Russians were equally guilty of spying on the USA. Khruschev promptly walked out of the summit.

1 January 1959: Fidel Castro announces the victory of the Cuban Revolution. American hostility to the new left-wing government was to turn Cuba into one of the hot-spots of the 1960s.

Gary Powers (sitting on the right in the box) on trial for espionage in Moscow in August 1960. This incident wrecked the thaw of 1959-60.

the USA. Plans were made for a summit in Paris in May 1960, but otherwise these visits produced nothing very concrete in the way of agreements on serious questions such as arms control, Berlin or the status of Communist China.

When an American U-2 spy plane was shot down over Soviet territory in May 1960, relations soured rapidly and the Paris Summit collapsed. The brief thaw was over.

The USA made her first successful hydrogen bomb test in 1953, the Soviet Union in 1954.

On 4 October 1957 Russia fired the first man-made satellite – the Sputnik – into orbit.

Much of this information was gathered from analysis of the effects of American atmospheric tests in the Pacific and Soviet ones in Siberia in 1954.

From a speech by President John F. Kennedy, made in 1962.

The Nuclear conundrum

During the 1950s nuclear weapons more sophisticated and deadly than the first atomic bomb were developed by both Superpowers, including a hydrogen bomb ten times more powerful than the Hiroshima device, intercontinental ballistic missiles (ICBMs) that could be fired directly at long-range targets, and the beginnings of a technology that would one day make it possible to launch weapons from outer space.

Each side was terrified that the other might draw ahead in nuclear technology and thus gain the upper hand in any war that might break out. At the same time, scientists were gathering more and more knowledge of the devastating effects of radiation on human tissue and the environment, forcing politicians to realize that 'we are rapidly getting to the point where no war can be won' (Eisenhower 1956). The logical way out of this impasse – negotiated agreements to put a brake on the development of new weapons (a test ban treaty) and to begin the dismantling of existing stockpiles (arms reduction) – was made impossible by the mutual distrust that existed even during the years of the thaw. Neither side would trust the other to keep to the terms of any agreement, and no mutually acceptable form of verification could be devised. At the 1955 Geneva Summit, Eisenhower made an imaginative attempt to overcome this problem with the Open Skies Plan, in which both nations would allow aerial overflights of their territory by the other. This was rejected by the Russians as too risky to their security.

In answer to this dilemma the American government adopted the doctrine of Mutually Assured Destruction, which critics noticed with grim humour could be abbreviated to 'MAD'. So long as the two Superpowers achieved a rough parity in the number and sophistication of their armaments, neither side, it was argued, would dare start a war, for the winner would suffer such devastation that any victory would be 'ashes in our mouths'. MAD meant, of course, a continuation of the arms race. By 1960 the Superpowers owned enough nuclear hardware between them to destroy the world ten times over.

Conclusion

By 1960 the Cold War dominated America's relations with the rest of the world. In spite of the verbal belligerency of Dulles, it was generally accepted that it was not feasible to roll back the 1947 frontiers of communism and that a direct confrontation between the Superpowers must be avoided at all costs. The risks were just too great. At the same time, the Truman Doctrine was in danger of turning the United States into the world's policeman and involving her with regimes that were little credit to the ideals of liberty and democracy in whose name the Cold War was being fought. And over everything hung the nuclear threat. Every new invention made a future war less winnable, yet rivalry between the Superpowers prevented not only arms reduction but even a freeze on any new developments.

3 THE AFFLUENT SOCIETY: THE USA AT HOME 1945~60

Post-war American society was affluent in a way no society had ever been affluent before. Pride in the success of the free enterprise system ran high. Beneath the surface, however, trouble brewed. Significant pockets of poverty still existed, and the civil rights issue was about to come to a head. Events were to show that civil liberties were under threat, not from external enemies but from forces inside the United States herself, who came close to destroying freedom in the name of defending it. And in the end, as the 1960s were to show, affluence bred a special set of problems all of its own.

Affluence and poverty

Source A
From *United States Statistical Abstracts* for 1945 and 1960.

	USA 1945	USA 1960 (population 179,323, 175 – 1960 Census)
Household television sets	7000	46,000,000
Domestic washing machines (automatic)	no statistics available	21,000,000
Households with one or more cars	20,000,000	41,000,000
Households with two or more cars	3,500,000	11,000,000
Annual sale of air-conditioners	11,000	1,580,000
College enrollments	1,555,599	3,500,000

Similar statistics for Britain and other West European nations, who are usually bracketed with the United States among the world's affluent industrial nations, are not readily available for this period. Only in 1964 did the Ministry of Labour in Britain judge that the possession of domestic labour-saving devices was spreading rapidly enough to make it worthwhile collecting figures. Even then, direct comparison with American figures is not possible. In 1964, 53 per cent of British households possessed a washing machine, but the Ministry survey makes no attempt to distinguish which type and hides the fact that the majority would have been rather primitive devices. There were few automatic washing machines in Britain in 1964 outside laundrettes and institutions.

Source B

From J. Guenther *Inside the USA* (1953 edition). Between 1947 and 1952 the author visited 48 states and all the major cities.

42 per cent of Kentucky farms are not reached by improved roads of any kind. Kentucky is the 47th state in literacy; only one other state (Mississippi) has more illiterates. 42,000 Kentucky farms have no toilets or privies of any kind, and 97 per cent of all farms have no toilets inside the house. Kentucky has the third highest death rate from tuberculosis, and in some areas a single doctor serves 11,500 people . . . . 37 per cent of Kentucky children fail to finish elementary school.

The average number of days a pupil goes to school in Kentucky is 129 (as against 150 for the country as a whole).

? ?

1 What do the statistics in source A tell us about changes in the American standard of living in the 1950s? What indications are there that US society is something quite unique?

2 It is not possible to make a point by point comparison but how does the overall picture of Kentucky in source B compare with the picture of the USA in source A? What explanations might there be for the discrepancy in the two sources?

3 The survival of poverty and injustice in America had little effect on the politics of the 1950s. What explanations might there be for this?

Among the fastest-growing cities was Seattle in Washington State, home of the Boeing Corporation, which built planes for the airforce and the new civilian airlines.

A man, for example, who had grown up in the Depression and left school without qualifications, might find an unskilled job in one of the new industries. With the high wages of the 1950s he could bring up his children in comfort and security and send them on to college to become doctors or lawyers, new members of the professional middle classes.

Between 1945 and 1960 the USA became a consumer society. Industries like those making electrical appliances, plastics, cars and business machines flourished, as did industries with defence contracts. Their well-paid workforces created a further demand for consumer goods and for services such as education and health care, which in turn generated more lucrative employment. At some time during that decade and a half most Americans climbed on to the bandwagon and were caught up in a cycle of affluence that worked in similar ways to the cycle of deprivation. The 'American dream' that with hard work anyone could attain security and prosperity for his family became fashionable again.

The Affluent Society. Outside a new out-of-town shopping mall stand rows of the gas-guzzling cars popular in the 1950s and 1960s.

The geographical distribution of the population changed. Businesses moved out of city centres into the suburbs, and their newly affluent employees moved with them, abandoning their apartments for houses and gardens. By 1960 63 per cent of Americans lived in suburbs. Other firms moved out of the old North-Eastern and Great Lakes industrial regions into the 'sunbelt' states of Florida, Texas, Arizona and California, whose populations rose by 140 per cent between 1940 and 1965.

About one-fifth of the American population was left out of this trend, including the farming communities of the Appalachian Mountain chain, which ran through West Virginia and Kentucky, and areas that were dependent on declining heavy industries like coal-mining and railways. Since the war, farming had become big business, and over six million small tenant farmers in the South and parts of the Mid-West, many of them black, were driven off the land between 1940 and 1964. Many migrated to the cities, where those who did not have the skills to find a foothold in the affluent society or who were excluded on grounds of race took up society's unwanted menial jobs and settled in inner city neighbourhoods vacated by the more prosperous. The centres of many Northern towns became ghettos of poverty.

When Senator John F. Kennedy visited West Virginia during the 1960 election campaign, he was so shocked by the poverty he saw there that one of his first acts on becoming President was to declare the region a deprived area eligible for federal aid.

For the fate of a small farmer in South Dakota, listen to the Bob Dylan song, 'The Ballad of Hollis Brown'.

Poverty in the midst of affluence. In this run-down house in the Appalachian Mountains lived a family of nine.

The Politics of the age

Truman began his presidency with a successful piece of Federal planning. The resettlement of veterans into civilian life was eased by the GI Bill of Rights, which gave ex-servicemen unemployment pay for a year, loans for the purchase of farms or businesses and generous grants to make up lost education.

For the rest of his first term Truman struggled. Although the country prospered, inflation and labour troubles dented his popularity. In Congress the Dixiecrats – alarmed by Truman's growing concern with civil rights – joined forces with the Republicans to obstruct his every move. It was widely predicted that he would lose the 1948 election to the Republican, Thomas E. Dewey.

Against all expectations, Truman was re-elected, and with a 21-point programme called 'The Fair Deal', presented to Congress on 5 January 1949, committed himself to federal activity as a cure for outstanding social and

These measures, plus the high wages paid to workers and servicemen during the war when there was little to spend them on, contributed to the post-war consumer boom by increasing the amount of money in circulation.

In the 1948 election, the Dixiecrats even split the Democratic Party by putting up their own anti-Truman candidate, Strom Thurmond of South Carolina.

economic problems. He specifically rejected the 'trickle down' theory of national prosperity and urged Americans to 'use our common resources to help one another in the hazzards and struggles of individual life'. Among the specific measures proposed were a national health service, a public housing programme, increased social security provision and a civil rights bill. These measures were once again obstructed by the Dixiecrat-Republican alliance. Republicans argued that welfare schemes would make people lazy and reduce the incentive to work. The country as a whole would become poorer rather than richer. Government supervision of businesses and individual lives would increase and would threaten civil liberties. Some even accused Truman of trying to introduce socialism by the back door.

In 1952 the Republican Dwight D. Eisenhower – 'Ike' – defeated the liberal Democratic candidate, Adlai Stevenson. There were a number of reasons for Ike's success, including his popularity as a successful wartime commander, Stevenson's denunciation of the then-popular Senator Joseph McCarthy, rumours of corruption in the White House and the stalemate in Korea. But, undoubtedly, Eisenhower also reflected something that the American people felt about the state of their own lives and futures. The majority of the electorate saw little advantage for themselves in federal activity to alleviate poverty, especially if it meant tax increases. They were doing well enough without help, and approved of Eisenhower's promise, made in his second State of the Union message on 7 January 1954, to lower taxes so that 'taxpayers may now spend their own money in their own way'.

Eisenhower was not a man of extremes. During his eight years as President (he was re-elected easily in 1956) some Republicans urged him to go the whole way and dismantle the welfare system of the New Deal. This Ike refused to do and he even extended the basic social security coverage to a further 10,000,000 workers and gave some aid to local authorities for slum clearance. The sweeping reforms of the Fair Deal, however, were forgotten, and for most of the 1950s the majority of Americans were happy that it should be so.

McCarthyism

The Truman years saw an outbreak of anti-Communist hysteria within the United States itself. It began in 1947 when the Senate Un-American Activities Committee started an investigation into the political affiliations of government employees, but erupted into a much more ugly phase in 1950 when Senator Joseph McCarthy of Wisconsin announced that he was in possession of the names of Communist sympathiziers inside the State Department (Foreign Office), who were trying to undermine the country from within. McCarthy was never able to substantiate his allegations, and at any other time might have been dismissed as a dangerous fraud. In 1950, however, the belief that all areas of American life had been infiltrated by 'subversives' caught hold of the popular imagination.

The background to this obsession is to be found in events abroad. To Americans, both simple and sophisticated, it seemed inconceivable that American superiority could be challenged – that Communists could come to power in China because they were genuninely more popular than the US-backed Nationalists, or that Soviet scientists were clever enough to develop an atomic bomb on their own. And, with the convictions of Alger Hiss and the Rosenbergs, there was just enough real evidence of subversion in America to give McCarthy credibility. Offering a simple answer to the complex problems of the modern world, he became for a time a sort of folk hero.

The anti-Communist crusade soon turned into a witch-hunt. To be found guilty the accused needed only to have Communist sympathies. It did not

There was not, and still is not, any national health service in America. All medical services are private and charge fees.

Eisenhower had been Supreme Commander of the Allied forces on D-Day, 6 June 1944, and Supreme Commander of NATO.

In a bestseller of 1958, *The Affluent Society*, the economist J.K. Galbraith pointed out that dire poverty still existed in the midst of American affluence. But now that the poor were a minority in society it was easy for public and politicians just to shut their eyes to the problem.

The number of secret Communists in the State Department given by McCarthy varied from speech to speech, from 57 to 205.

Hiss, a minor State Department official, was found guilty in 1950 of lying about his connections with the Russians in the 1930s. Ethel and Julius Rosenberg were executed for passing on atomic secrets to the Russians.

Among the more ludicrous cases was that of a soldier who was forced to undergo a security clearance because of the political past of his mother-in-law, who had died ten years before he met his wife.

During the war, when Russia was America's ally, a series of films had been made glorifying the Soviet war-effort. This led to the persecution of many Hollywood actors and film-makers. Charlie Chaplin was so outraged by his treatment that he left America, vowing never to return.

need to be proved that he had actually *done* anything disloyal. Soon suspicion fell not only on people with Communist connections, however vague, but on anyone whose commitment to a fanatical anti-Communism was less than 100 per cent. These included Robert Oppenheimer, leader of the team that invented the first atomic bomb, who had expressed doubts about the morality of the hydrogen bomb; and George Marshall, who had tried to mediate in 1946 between the Chinese Communists and Nationalists. Every non-conformist – including Quakers, homosexuals, academics who specialized in Russian culture or Marxism – whose lifestyle was different from his neighbour's became fair game. The Un-American Activities Committee had no power to send the convicted to gaol but it could imprison those who refused to appear before it for 'contempt'. Many reputations were ruined, causing a number of suicides. In the 1952 election campaign Eisenhower refused to speak out against McCarthy and chose as his Vice-President Richard M. Nixon, who had played a leading role in investigating and prosecuting Alger Hiss. This implied agreement with McCarthyism won the General many votes.

Source A

Extracts from six pamphlets published by the Un-American Activities Committee between 1947 and 1952, entitled *100 Things you should know about Communism in the USA*. Over one million of these pamphlets were either sold or given away.

Hoover was head of the FBI 1924-72.

Q. Where can a Communist be found in everyday American life?
A. Look for him in your school, your labor union or your civic club. Communists themselves say that they can be found 'on almost any conceivable battlefront for the human mind'.

Q. Are there Communist clergymen?
A. Unfortunately, yes.

Q. But is Communism a real danger inside our churches?
A. Here's J. Edgar Hoover on the subject: 'I confess to a real apprehension, so long as the Communists are able to secure ministers of the gospel to promote their evil work and espouse a cause that is so alien to the religion of Christ and Judaism.'

Q. Do many of our teachers play the Communist game?
A. The files of our committee, running back over a ten-year period, show that the Communists have always found the teaching group the easiest touch of all the professional classes . . .

Q. Can you say some Communists have sneaked into our Government today?
A. Yes. And we repeat, nobody knows how many.

Q. Would anyone but a fool be willing to spy for Russia?
A. No. But you'll find 'fools' in pretty HIGH places. Soviet spy rings contain well-educated and able Americans who are looked up to by their fellow men. They may be scientists, lawyers, professors, writers, Government career workers, and even successful businessmen who have been filled with Communist poison.

Source B

From a speech by President Truman to the American Legion, 1950. Truman's dislike of McCarthyism won him McCarthy's emnity. After he left office, a number of people who had worked for him, especially on Fair Deal measures or in negotiations with the Russians or Chinese, were indicted before the Committee.

Disaffection: disloyalty.

Slander, lies, character assassination – these things are a threat to every single citizen everywhere in this country. When even one American – who has done nothing wrong – is forced by fear to shut his mind and close his mouth, then all Americans are in peril. It is the job of all of us – of every American who loves his country and his freedom – to rise up and put a stop to this terrible business . . . . A community may already be in the process of dissolution when each man begins to eye his neighbour as a possible enemy, where non-conformity with the accepted creed . . . is a mark of disaffection; where denunciation without specification or backing takes the place of evidence.

? ?

1 What aspects of McCarthyism does Truman denounce in source B?

2 Examine the extracts from the pamphlets in source A. What proof do they give of Communist infiltration or real help in identifying Communists? What

sort of behaviour do these pamphlets encourage? Do they bear out Truman's fears?

3 In what ways does the behaviour encouraged by McCarthyism contradict those principles for which American society is supposed to stand? Is there a warning here for all democratic societies?

In the end, the McCarthy spell was broken. In the spring of 1954 Committee proceedings began to be televised and McCarthy's bullying tactics and reliance on unsubstantiated allegations were made glaringly obvious to 20 million viewers. At the same time he turned his attention to the army, and when he accused General MacArthur of Communist sympathies he lost all credibility. In December, the Senate passed a vote of censure against him and he was finished.

He died in 1957.

Senator Joseph McCarthy in action during the McCarthy-army hearings in 1954.

The battle for civil rights: the first stage

Opposition from the Dixiecrats meant that Truman was unable to get a single item of his civil rights legislation through Congress, although, using his powers as Commander-in-Chief, he desegregated the armed forces in 1948. It was left to the Supreme Court to make the first move, when it ruled in 1954 that 'in the field of public education the doctrine of separate but equal has no place. Separate educional facilities are inherently unequal'.

This was the final judgment in the case of Brown v. the Board of Education of Topeka, Kansas. It had been brought by the parents of Lynda Brown, a black girl who had been refused entry to the local all-white school.

In the years after this ruling, however, the Southern states made little effort to comply with it, nor the federal government to enforce it. It was in these circumstances that the negro civil rights movement was born.

Source A

Eisenhower, 1954, in a private conversation with Attorney-General Brownall.

I am convinced that the Supreme Court decision sets back progress in the South for at least fifteen years. It's all very well to talk about school integration – if you remember you may also be talking about social disintegration. Feelings are deep on this . . . . And the fellows who try to tell you that you can do these things by force are just plain nuts.

Source B

From a speech by the Revd. Martin Luther King Jr. on 6 December 1955 announcing the Montgomery (Alabama) bus boycott. The occasion for this protest was an incident in which a black seamstress, Mrs Rosa Parks, was ordered to give up her seat on a bus to a white man. She refused and was arrested. For a whole year, until December 1956, the Blacks of Montgomery boycotted the buses and brought the bus company to the verge of bankruptcy.

There comes a time when people get tired. We are here this evening to say to those who have mistreated us so long that we are tired – tired of being segregated and humiliated, tired of being kicked about by the brutal feet of oppression. We have no alternative but to protest . . . . We are impatient for justice but we will protest with love. There will be no violence on our part. . . . If you will, protest courageously and yet with dignity and Christian love, when the history books are written in future generations, the historians will have to pause and say, 'There lived a great people – a black people – who injected new meaning and dignity into the veins of civilization'.

? ?

1 On what grounds does Eisenhower think that the 1954 court decision is both dangerous and impractical?

2 About what and with whom are the Montgomery Blacks angry in 1955? They have endured humiliation for years; why is it now that their anger erupts?

3 What particular form of protest does King advocate? What might his reasons be for choosing such a form?

Federal paratroopers escort black students into school at the height of the Little Rock crisis, September 1957.

The main civil rights organizations were the Southern Christian Leadership Conference (SCLC), led by Martin Luther King; the Students' Non-Violent Co-ordinating Committee (SNCC); and the Commission for Racial Equality (CORE).

In February 1960 some Blacks began a sit-in at Woolworth's segregated lunch counter in Greensboro, North Carolina, when they had been refused service. Led by the SNCC, the movement spread rapidly throughout the South.

By the historian, Arthur M. Schlesinger, in conversation with John A. Garraty and quoted in J.A. Garraty *Interpreting American History* (1970).

Another book that made an impact on the national mood was Michael Harrington's *The Other America* (1962), which was the inspiration behind President Johnson's 'War on Poverty', a series of federal programmes announced by President Johnson in 1964 to wipe out the causes and effects of poverty in America (see p. 27).

Tired of waiting for governments to act, Southern Blacks took matters into their own hands. By peaceful protest, they hoped to awaken the conscience of the nation and prove to businesses that segregation was economically damaging. Their goal was full integration into all areas of American life, and their first great success was the desegregation of the Montgomery city buses in December 1956.

A few courageous black students started to demand their legal right of access to white schools. When nine of them tried to enrol at the Central High School in Little Rock, Arkansas, in 1957, they were stopped by a mob of angry white citizens. The state police just stood idly by, and Eisenhower was at last compelled to intervene, not on the grounds of morality or justice but because the Arkansas state Government was openly flouting the law and being seen to do so by millions of television viewers throughout the world. Federal paratroopers were sent to escort the black children into school.

By 1960 only a limited amount of progress had been made. There was some patchy desegregation of businesses and local services, but 90 per cent of the South's black children still attended segregated schools, and in the 1960 election only 15 per cent of Blacks in the South voted. The mood of Blacks had been changed for good, however, and the early months of 1960 were to mark the beginning of the highpoint of the black struggle for civil rights.

Conclusion

Contemporaries often complained that Americans of the 1950s were complacent and selfish. It is hardly surprising, therefore, that the reforming zeal of the 1930s and 1940s fizzled out or that the undynamic Ike was twice elected President. It has been suggested that the great social problems of the 1960s and 1970s – the decay of the inner cities and the alienation of black youth – might never have reached crisis-point if they had been tackled at this earlier stage.

By the end of the decade, in the aftermath of Galbraith's book *The Affluent Society*, there were signs that the national mood was changing, especially among the young. Part of the attraction of the 1960 Democratic Presidential candidate, John F. Kennedy, lay in his appeal to latent idealism and social conscience.

In the 1950s the mood of the nation had been most disturbed by events abroad. Americans had shown how easily a sophisticated people could fall prey to the mass intolerance and hysteria of McCarthyism. It is a tribute to the strength of the US political system and the good sense of her people that sanity eventually prevailed.

4 COMING APART:
THE USA IN THE 1960S

From W.L. O'Neill *Coming Apart: an Unofficial History of the United States in the 1960s* (1971).

Presidents:
John F. Kennedy 1960-3
Lyndon B. Johnson 1963-8
Richard M. Nixon 1968-74

There is no better way to capture the new mood of restlessness and expectation than in the ringing phrases of Kennedy's inaugural speech (20 January 1961):

Man holds in his mortal hands the power to abolish all forms of human poverty and all forms of human life.

If a free society cannot help the many who are poor, it cannot save the few who are rich.

And so, my fellow Americans, ask not what your country can do for you, ask what you can do for your country.

The idea, fashionable in 1960, that social injustice and poverty could be eradicated by policies that most reasonable Americans could agree with was known as 'concensus politics'.

There seemed no limit to what the United States, with her vast natural and human resources, could achieve, both at home and abroad, if only the will were there. Kennedy's election was greeted with an upsurge of excitement and enthusiasm.

The Men of the Decade

John F. Kennedy

At 43 Kennedy was the youngest man ever elected as President of the United States.

Kennedy's record as a senator for Massachusetts had been undistinguished; and until 1960 he had not been widely known to the public. Once in office, he announced a programme of social reform called the New Frontier, which included a Medicare scheme to provide subsidized health care for the elderly, and federal aid to education. He achieved little, however, for few of his measures managed to pass through Congress. On civil rights his stand was ambiguous. Although personally sympathetic to the plight of Blacks, as an ambitious politician he could not forget how unpopular a civil rights bill would be in the South. It was not until June 1963 that he finally made up his mind to act and presented Congress with a draft bill totally banning segregation in education and in public places. This bill had made little progress by the time Kennedy was assassinated in Dallas, Texas, on 22 November 1963. Lee Harvey Oswald was charged with the murder but was himself killed before he could be brought to trial.

Between 1960 and 1963 activity by black civil rights movements reached its height (see p. 27).

The Kennedy charisma – on the campaign trail in 1960. Kennedy had the art of making people believe in him, but the debate over how good a President he really was still goes on.

A photograph taken at the actual moment of Kennedy's assassination. In the back seat of the car, the President slumps forward after being shot in the head.

President Johnson set up the Warren Commission to investigate the assassination. It concluded that Kennedy had been shot by a lone gunman, Oswald. Serious doubts have since been raised about the Commission's findings, and a question mark still hangs over the issue of who killed Kennedy.

Abroad, Kennedy continued the policy of containment, founded the Peace Corps to send volunteers to do community work in the Third World and began the fatal stepping-up of the American commitment to South Vietnam (see p. 36). He is best-remembered for his show-down with the Russians during the Cuban Missile Crisis of 1962 (see p. 33) and for the thaw in East-West relations that followed.

Both before and after his death, Kennedy was adored and admired by many, inside and outside America, as the one man who might, had he lived long enough, have dampened down the Cold War, achieved a meaningful degree of disarmament, restored America's status in the Third World and brought justice to Blacks and relief to the poor. When he died, the optimism of millions of Americans died with him. In recent years this heroic reputation has been questioned. Critics have pointed out that Kennedy was more of a reluctant follower than a leader in civil rights matters, that he brought America to the brink of a major war in 1962 and that he drew her deeper into the quagmire that was Vietnam. Kennedy's reputation, according to one historian, depended mainly on his charisma and clever public relations, by which his administration:

B. Miroff, *Pragmatic Illusions*, 1976.

. . . managed to convince much of the nation that it represented genuine novelty in American political life, when what it really represented were tired clichés in vinyl wrappings.

Lyndon B. Johnson

As Kennedy's Vice-President, Johnson came to office suddenly and unexpectedly. He was elected in his own right in 1964. Although a Southerner from Texas, he was a liberal and continued Kennedy's reform programme. In this Johnson was far more successful than Kennedy himself had been, for he was a skilful manipulator of Congress and was able to take advantage of the wave of shock that shook the country after Kennedy's death. He called his programme the Great Society, and in the course of two years – 1964 and 1965 – passed more measures than Franklin Roosevelt had done in a comparable period of time, including a civil rights bill, the Voting Rights Act, a Medicare

Before becoming Vice-President, Johnson had been Democratic-leader in the Senate.

The Voting Rights Act appointed federal officials to supervise elections in the South, and banned literacy tests.

A broken man, President Johnson announces that he will not run for re-election, April 1968.

One agency of the War on Poverty was the Head Start Project, to provide pre-school education for deprived under-fives. The television show 'Sesame Street' was an offshoot of this scheme.

In 1968 Johnson's security men told him that they could not guarantee his safety anywhere outside military bases.

Professor Rossiter of Cornell University in an article on President Johnson in *Time* magazine, 5 January 1968.

For example, during the 'Freedom Rides' of 1961 civil rights workers, black and white, had travelled across the South on interstate transport, deliberately ignoring segregated seating arrangements, lavatories, canteens etc. In 1962 all interstate terminals were desegregated.

scheme, and federal aid to education, housing and the arts. A 'War on Poverty' programme broke new ground by giving money directly to needy communities to spend in American cities as they saw fit.

In 1964, American commitment to Vietnam, which Johnson had not started but which he stepped up, drew her into a full-scale war. By 1968 this war was so unpopular that many Americans had begun to question the wisdom of the whole policy of Containment, and Johnson had become one of the most unpopular presidents of modern times. 'LBJ, LBJ' shouted the demonstrators every time he appeared in public, 'how many kids have you killed today?'. The Great Society itself was a casualty of the war. As all available funds were sucked into the war effort, existing domestic programmes were cut and no new ones were initiated after 1965. By 1968 Johnson's reputation was over-shadowed by the war and, a broken man, he decided not to run for re-election.

Johnson left office an unlamented, and even a hated, President. With the passing of time, however, it has become possible to judge his presidency as a whole and not merely in the light of the Vietnam tragedy. Many would now agree with the words of a contemporary, written in January 1968:

Before Vietnam took the centre of the stage, Lyndon Johnson would have ranked with what we call the first-class second-class Presidents, and perhaps with a big effort even rise above that . . . . This war has damaged Lyndon Johnson's place in history.

The crisis of civil rights

In the first half of the 1960s the black civil rights movement succeeded in dismantling much of the apparatus of segregation in the South. Courageous individuals like James Meredith, who enrolled at the all-white Mississippi State University in 1962, became internationally known figures. In August 1963, 200,000 gathered for a civil rights demonstration at the Lincoln Memorial in Washington, at which Martin Luther King spoke of his dream of a colour-blind America. In 1964 and 1965 two important civil rights measures were passed by Congress (see p. 26).

Although many ingenious devices were invented by Southerners to evade the new laws, much was achieved. Within two years of the enactment of the Voting Rights Act, black voter registration had gone up from 6.7 per cent to 59.8 per cent in Mississippi and from 19.3 per cent to 51.6 per cent in Alabama. By 1970 most Southern schools had been integrated.

Soldiers of the California National Guard stand ready for action on a nearly deserted street in the Watts area of Los Angeles after several days of rioting.

In Los Angeles black unemployment was over 30 per cent.

In Memphis, Tennessee, by a white man, James Earl Ray.

Source A

From *What We Want* by Stokeley Carmichael, published in the *New York Review of Books*, 22 September 1966. Carmichael was a member of SNCC (see p. 24).

This was the origin of the idea of 'Black Power'. Carmichael meant that black communities should organize themselves to win political power in their own communities. Other black groups interpreted it differently, but all tried to teach Negroes to have pride in their racial heritage – 'Black is Beautiful' was the slogan. It was at this time that Negroes began calling themselves 'Blacks' as a term of pride.

Source B

From the Massey Lectures given by Martin Luther King in 1967 for the Canadian Broadcasting Corporation.

In the light of these achievements many Americans were bewildered when violent rioting broke out in the Watts suburb of Los Angeles in August 1965. Over the next four 'long hot summers' of 1966-9 rioting occurred in more than 40 cities, including New York, Chicago, Cincinnati and Detroit. In the outbreak of violence following the assassination of Martin Luther King in April 1968 rioting reached to within two blocks of the White House itself. The inner city riots were mostly spontaneous and unorganized and expressed the deep frustrations still remaining in black society. It had soon become obvious that the successful civil rights battle had done little to improve the lives of Northern Blacks trapped in the cycle of deprivation, and many Blacks suspected that Northern Whites would fight as hard to retain their economic and social superiority as Southerners had once fought to defend segregation. Black leaders were forced to rethink their goals and methods, and the civil rights movement split.

After years . . . we are almost at the same point – because we demonstrated from a point of weakness. We cannot be expected any longer to march and have our heads broken in order to say to Whites: 'Come on, you're nice guys.' For you are not nice guys. We have found you out . . . .

We have to work for power because this country does not function by morality, love and non-violence, but by power. Thus we are determined to win political power, with the idea of moving on from there into activity that would have economic effects. With power, the masses could make . . . the decisions which govern their destinies and thus create basic change in their day-to-day lives . . . .

He [a black man] may also need a gun, and SNCC reaffirms the right of black men everywhere to defend themselves when threatened or attacked. As for initiating violence, we hope that such programmes as ours will make that unnecessary; but it is not for us to tell black communities whether they can or cannot use any particular form of action to resolve their problems. Responsibility for the use of violence by black men, whether in self-defence or initiated by them, lies with the white community.

As elation [at the success of the civil rights movement in the South] . . . died, Negroes became sharply aware that the goal of freedom was still distant and our immediate plight was still substantially an agony of deprivation. In the past decade little had been done for the Northern ghettos. All the legislation was designed to remedy the Southern situation . . . .

To achieve justice, Negroes . . . must fashion new tactics, which do not count on Government goodwill but serve, instead, to compel unwilling authorities to yield to the mandates of justice . . . .

King advocated black non-co-operation with city authorities – eg. non payment of taxes, boycotts, sit-ins and strikes.

Catharsis: emotional release

I am still convinced that a solution of non-violence remains possible. However, non-violence must be adapted to urban conditions and urban moods . . . . Mass civil disobedience as a new stage of struggle can transmute the deep rage of the ghetto into a constructive and creative force. To dislocate the functioning of a city without destroying it can be more effective than a riot because it can be longer lasting, costly to the larger society, but not wantonly destructive. Finally it is a device of social action that is more difficult for the government to quell by superior force.

The limitation of riots, moral questions aside, is that they cannot win, and their participants know it . . . . It involves an emotional catharsis but it must be followed by a sense of futility.

? ?

1 In what ways do King and Carmichael's assessments of the black position by the mid-1960s coincide?

2 What major difference is there between them on the question of tactics? What arguments would they use to justify their respective positions?

3 To what extent have the aims and methods of both King and Carmichael altered since the early 1960s? What developments have caused them to change?

The revolt of the young

The number of college enrollments rose again from 3.8 to 6.5 million in the 1960s.

In the summer of 1964 – 'Freedom Summer' – thousands of Northern college students took part in a voter registration campaign in Mississippi in the teeth of violent opposition from local Whites.

The changes in behaviour among the young, especially sexual behaviour, were labelled the 'Permissive Society' by the older generation.

For a contemporary picture of the counter-culture, read *The Greening of America* by Charles Reich (1970). The author gathered much of his material by talking to students in the dining hall at Havard, and predicted – wrongly, as it turned out – that the new consciousness would permanently transform the USA.

By 1964 there were 13 million more Americans between the ages of 14 and 24 than there had been in 1950. Most had grown up in unprecedented affluence and were better educated than ever before. If youth had been complacent and conformist in the 1950s, this was certainly no longer true by 1960. Kennedy's call to Americans to put their affluence at the service of their fellow men tapped a well of idealism in the young. They joined the civil rights movement and the Peace Corps in increasing numbers. At the same time, many began to question the values by which they had been brought up and to experiment with new lifestyles, abandoning long-standing conventions in dress, language and social and sexual behaviour.

By the middle of the decade disillusion had set in. Many young people came to the conclusion that American society was not worth reforming but should be destroyed and replaced with something new and more genuinely egalitarian, although the actual form this would take was usually left very vague. The universities became hotbeds of political radicalism and attacked the hated symbols of a corrupt society – banks, industries that took contracts from the Pentagon (Defence Department), the universities themselves. Between 1964 and 1970 many major colleges like Berkeley, California, and Columbia, New York, almost ceased to function as teaching institutions.

Other disaffected young people found a more personal solution, dropping out of society altogether into the counter-culture of the hippies. By changing the way individuals related to each other, especially when aided by mind-altering drugs like marijuana ('pot', 'hashish', 'grass') and LSD, they hoped that society as a whole could be transformed, and status-seeking, rivalry and greed for material possessions would be replaced by love and co-operation. Whole areas of big cities like Haight Ashbury in San Francisco and the East Village in New York changed their character overnight as the hippies moved in.

The Vietnam War was hated everywhere. Militant students mobbed pro-war politicians. Thousands burnt their draft-cards or fled abroad to avoid the call-up.

To many it seemed as if the prediction of the folk-singer, Bob Dylan, that

The California National Guard are called out again, here to disperse student protests on Berkeley campus. The guardsmen are wearing masks in case they need to use tear gas. The universities were at the centre of youthful rebellion against society.

From 'The Times They Are A' Changin'', 1965.

Source A

From the testimony of Tom Hayden, leader of one student radical group, the SDS (Students for a Democratic Society), before the Senate Commission investigating the riots at the 1968 Democratic Party convention at Chicago, where anti-war demonstrators and police clashed violently.

Status quo: the situation as it exists.

The voting age in 1968 was 21. It was lowered to 18 in 1971.

Draft: conscription into the US army.

'your sons and your daughters are beyond your command' was indeed coming true and that American society, which had appeared so stable at the beginning of the decade, was coming apart.

In Vietnam we saw an international dimension to the violence and racism we were already seeing at home. I want to remind the commission that the anti-war movement began with the premise that Vietnam was a mistake that could be brought to the attention of the government, that legal and conventional channels were available that could be used . . . . Our foreign policy officials were invited to the universities. They participated in teach-ins. The reason that they don't go to the major universities any more is not because we have run them away, but because they know they have nothing to say.

Moreover, our own professors were using their so-called academic freedom to perfect methods of torture, methods of chemical and biological warfare . . . . From the viewpoint of America's rulers, apparently, the universities are indispensable to the modern military effort, and students must be trained to accept the status quo and carry it on . . . .

Look at the situation of a student facing this problem. He has no vote. His voice does not count . . . . Attempts to work within the system have been frustrated, and the student is not able to ignore the war for two basic reasons . . . first the draft, and second the transformation of the university into an instrument of American foreign policy . . . . For many students the draft represents the most tangible form of oppression they have experienced in their sheltered middle-class lives.

So, what I am saying is that the student movement . . . was becoming more radical basically because of its experience in this society. From a position of expecting idealistically that the authorities would listen to us, we were moving towards questioning the legitimacy of authority . . . towards confrontation.

Source B

From the testimony of Father Andrew Greely, a Roman Catholic priest from Chicago, to the National Opinion Research Centre, 1968.

Ethnics were the descendants of immigrants of East European, Irish and Italian extraction, who tended to live in close-knit communities and be employed mainly in blue-collar jobs. They were firmly attached to the values of family life and the Church, and together with traditionally conservative rural Americans, were often labelled 'Middle America'.

In the eyes of the white ethnic, 'peace' has been identified as a 'radical' cause. The ethnics want no part of contemporary radicalism, especially when it is advocated by long-haired college students . . . . However moral and virtuous the present radical movement may be, it has turned off between 60 and 70 per cent of the American population. If the white ethnic is told in effect that to support peace he must also support the Black Panthers, women's liberation, wide-spread use of drugs, free love, campus radicals, **Dr Spock** [the well-known child care expert, who was tried in 1968 for helping draft-dodgers], long hair and picketing clergymen, he may find it very difficult to put himself on the side of peace.

???

1 Why, according to Hayden in source A, have American students decided that American society and government are rotten to the core?

2 What does source B tell us about American society in the late 1960s which it would be easy to miss given all the attention paid by the media to the young radicals?

3 The student rebels and the conservative ethnics came, on the whole, from different social groups and had different life experiences. Why should each group react in such a way at such a time, and what did each feel they had to lose or gain? (This is a question to which there is no one simple answer.)

The race for the moon

In April 1961 the Russians scored another 'first' when they put the first human being, Yuri Gagarin, into orbit around the earth. A month later President Kennedy asked Congress to finance a $24,000 million programme to enable the USA to achieve 'the goal, before this decade is out, of landing a man on the moon and returning him safely to earth'. In February 1962 John Glenn duly became the first American to orbit the earth, and on 20 July 1969 the first moonlanding took place.

By the astronauts, Neil Armstrong and 'Buzz' Aldrin in Apollo 11.

Cold War rivalry was obviously one incentive for the space race, but there were other equally important if less tangible reasons. The space programme was, above all, the child of the optimistic early 1960s. Ten years later it might not even have got started.

Source A

From President Kennedy's speech to Congress, May 1961.

We choose to go to the moon. We choose to go to the moon in this decade and do the other things, not because they are easy but because they are hard; because that goal will serve to organize and measure the best of our energies and skills; because the challenge is one that we are willing to accept, one we are unwilling to postpone, and one which we intend to win.

From a letter to *Time*, 7 January 1969, referring to the Apollo 8 mission which circumnavigated the moon as a prelude to the actual moon-landing later that year.

We needed that. The three brave men, flying further and faster to more forbidding frontiers than ever before, are an inspiration we have needed and must not let slip. In tormented 1968, symbols of pride and constructive achievement were singularly lacking in our national life, but such inspiration might be just what we need to urge us to work harder, moan less and move into 1969 with a new resolve to overcome our earth-bound problems.

The first man on the moon: Astronaut Neil Armstrong in July 1969.

??

1 In what way are Kennedy's motives for launching the moon project symptomatic of America in the early 1960s?

2 What events have been taking place in the USA in the months before the letter in source B was written? In what way might this letter be said to reflect the changed mood of America in the late 1960s?

Conclusion: America at the end of the decade

At the beginning of the 1960s few Americans could have predicted the startling course the decade would take. By 1970 the liberal dream of 1960 that the USA had the resources and the will to root out poverty and injustice by consensus politics was in tatters. Much of society was bitterly divided between those who believed that justice could only be achieved by revolution, either political or personal, and those whose distaste for some or all of the trends of the later 1960s was so great that they longed to turn back the clock to a more orderly and traditional way of life. With the assassinations of Robert Kennedy and Martin Luther King in 1968 violence seemed to have become an endemic part of politics. Over all hung the shadow of the Vietnam War, which had begun as just one more war of Containment and had grown into a mighty hurricane that broke political reputations and set one American against another.

In the 1968 presidential election the Democrat, Hubert Humphrey, who had been Johnson's Vice-President and was tarred with his unpopularity, ran against the Republican, Richard M. Nixon. Nixon promised to take America out of Vietnam and restore law and order at home and the old-fashioned values of the 'silent majority', who opposed drugs, violent protest and the permissive society. Nixon beat Humphrey by a narrow margin (31.8 million votes to 31.3 million), revealing the deep gulf between the radicals, black and white, who enjoyed a lion's share of the news coverage in 1968, and conservative Middle America, whose numbers were great enough to sway the election result.

The divisions in American society tended to obscure the fact that considerable progress had been made both in achieving civil rights and eradicating poverty. The number of Americans living below the poverty line was halved between 1959 and 1969, although intractable pockets of urban and rural poverty did remain (see p. 19).

THE CRISIS OF CONTAINMENT: THE USA AND THE WORLD 1960~70

In 1960 American policy-makers had more questions than answers. Relations with the Soviet Union were frostier than they had been for several years and no progress had yet been made towards limiting the costly and perilous arms race. The Containment policy, which few questioned in principle, was spreading America's commitments worldwide and involving her with some unsavoury regimes.

The Cuban Missile Crisis

During his lifetime Kennedy brought hope to many that the tensions of the Cold War might be permanently eased, and the belief that things might have been different had he lived longer lingered on after his death.

During the first two years of his presidency, however, the Cold War intensified. Alarmed by reports of a 'missile gap', Kennedy ordered a build-up of long-range nuclear weapons, which provoked the Soviet Union into resuming atmospheric testing in September 1961. The USA followed suit in April 1962. Kennedy continued Eisenhower's implacable hostility to Castro's government in Cuba. Castro was left-wing – one of his earliest actions was to nationalize the American sugar companies in Cuba – but not yet officially a Communist. The United States retaliated with a boycott on Cuban sugar, and from then on Castro grew closer to the Russians. In April 1961 Kennedy authorized an invasion of the island by CIA-trained and -equipped anti-Castro Cuban exiles. This force was soundly beaten at the Bay of Pigs, a humiliating defeat for the new President.

In October 1962, Kennedy came closer than any President before him to a face-to-face showdown with the Russians. During a routine espionage flight over Cuba, Soviet ICBMs, which were not yet operational, were discovered. For six days, from 16 to 22 October, Kennedy and his advisers debated behind closed doors over what they should do next.

There were three main options: to do nothing except protest verbally; to invade Cuba by land or air and destroy the missile sites; or to find some third alternative that would avoid the risks of the first two.

Castro had seized power in January 1959, overthrowing the US-backed dictatorship of Batista.

It is possible, although not provable, that this might not have happened had America followed a less negative policy towards Cuba.

These missiles were capable of hitting most of the major cities of North and South America. It was estimated that within a few minutes of their being fired 80 million Americans would be dead.

Source A
From President Kennedy's television speech to the nation, 22 October 1962.

Neither the United States of America nor the world community of nations can tolerate deliberate deception and offensive threats on the part of any nation, large or small . . .
. . . this secret, swift and extraordinary build-up of Communist missiles . . . is a deliberately provocative and unjustified change in the status quo which cannot be accepted by this country if our courage and commitment are ever to be trusted again by friend or foe.

The 1930s taught us a clear lesson: aggressive conduct, if allowed to go unchecked and unchallenged, ultimately leads to war .... Our unswerving objective, therefore, must be to prevent the use of these missiles against this or any other country, and to secure their withdrawal or elimination from the Western Hemisphere.

He [Robert Kennedy] thought it would be very, very difficult indeed for the President if the decision were to be for an airstrike, with all the memory of Pearl Harbour and with all the implications this would have for us in whatever world there would be afterward .... A sneak attack was not in our traditions. Thousands of Cubans would be killed without warning and a lot of Russians too. He favoured *action*, to make known immediately the seriousness of the United States determination to get the missiles out of Cuba, but he thought the action should allow the Soviets some room for manoeuvre to pull back from their over-extended position in Cuba.

Source B
An account by Leonard C. Meeker, deputy legal adviser at the State Department, of a conversation with Robert Kennedy, the President's brother and a member of the crisis team, during the week of 16-22 October.

? ?

1 What does President Kennedy think must happen to the missiles and what two reasons does he give for his opinion? Why does Kennedy make a reference to the 1930s here?

2 What reason does Robert Kennedy give for rejecting the airstrike option and what has the reference to Pearl Harbour to do with it? What other, unspoken reason does he hint at in lines 3-4?

3 What conditions does Robert Kennedy set out for any policy that is to be adopted? Does the quarantine option (see below) fit these conditions?

The Soviet ship Divinogorsk *carrying two canvas-covered missiles, en route for Cuba in October 1962. If the Soviet ships had not turned back, the consequences for world peace would have been incalculable.*

In October 1964 Khruschev was removed from office by the Politburo (the council of top Communist Party leaders who govern the USSR). It is possible, though not yet provable, that one of the reasons

It was finally decided to throw a naval blockade or 'quarantine' around Cuba to prevent Soviet ships carrying parts to complete the missile bases reaching the island. This might convince Khruschev of US determination to remove the missiles, while at the same time giving him a breathing space to rethink and climb down without undue humiliation. It was a risky strategy. If the Soviet

for this was that some senior Soviet politicians thought that he had been too 'soft' during the missile crisis. He was replaced by the joint leadership of Leonid Brezhnev and Alexei Kosygin.

ships defied the blockade Kennedy would either have to climb down himself or fight a naval battle with the Russians. After the decision was announced on American television on the evening of Monday 22 October, the world held its breath. After six days of unprecedented tension, Khruschev agreed to dismantle the missiles and the crisis was over.

The aftermath of the Missile Crisis

Kennedy forbade any gloating over the American 'victory', and the crisis did not worsen but improved relations between the Superpowers. Both leaders realized how close they had come to a major war and began to rethink their attitudes. In June 1963 the Hot Line, a direct telex link between the Kremlin and the White House, was set up so that the leaders could communicate directly during a crisis and minimize the risk of war by misunderstanding. Negotiations began for a test ban treaty, which, however, soon became bogged down in arguments with the Russians over verification and with American politicians over the extent to which the Russians could be trusted to keep any agreement.

Verification: the ability of each side to prove that the other had indeed carried out its promises.

Source A
From a speech by Republican Senator Barry Goldwater, 1963.

I see in our history, that what peace we have had has been possible because of strength. I see no change in the future until or unless the objectives of communism, not just their weapons, change.

Source B
From a letter to *Time*, June 1963.

Lest we forget: on May 17 1933 Adolf Hitler delivered his famous 'Peace Speech', a masterpiece of deceptive propaganda that proclaimed Germany's wish for disarmament. There was great rejoicing throughout the Western world at this unexpected reasonableness, but in reality Hitler's plan was to give the world a false sense of security while secretly building up Germany's forces.
   Let us hope that history is not repeating itself in our new-found Russian 'friends'.

Source C
From a speech made by President Kennedy at the American University in Washington, 10 June 1963.

Some say that it is useless to speak of world peace . . . or world disarmament – and that it will be useless until the leaders of the Soviet Union adopt a more enlightened attitude. I hope they do. I believe we can help them to do it. But I also believe that we must examine our own attitudes – as individuals and as a nation – for our attitude is as essential as their's . . . .
   [The American people must be careful] not to see only a distorted and desperate view of the other side, not to see conflict as inevitable, accommodation as impossible, and communication as nothing more than an exchange of threats . . . . If we cannot now end our difference, at least we can help make the world safe for diversity. For, in the final analysis, our most common basic link is that we all inhabit this small planet. We all breathe the same air. We all cherish our children's future. And we are all mortal.

? ?

1 What is the attitude of the authors of sources A and B towards any agreement with the Russians? What reasons do they give for their attitude?

2 In what way does Kennedy's attitude towards the Russians, as expressed in source C, differ from the first two?

3 What motives might Kennedy have had for making such a speech at such a time? Does this speech (and Kennedy's behaviour after October 1962) justify his reputation as the man who might have turned the Cold War around? This is a tricky question and the answer to it will never be known for certain. Think about it as you study the rest of the decade.

The only other progress made during the 1960s was the 1968 Non-Proliferation Treaty, which aimed to limit the spread of nuclear knowledge beyond those nations already in possession of it.

In 1963 the world was shocked by pictures of Buddhist monks setting fire to themselves in protest against Diem. In October of that year Diem was overthrown by his own army officers. The US ambassador in Saigon, Henry Cabot Lodge, knew about and even encouraged the plot in the hope that it might produce a genuinely popular government and ease American qualms about her involvement. It did not.

The Senate voted 98 to 2 in favour, the only objectors being Senators Fulbright of Arkansas and Morse of Oregon. It was later revealed by the Pentagon Papers (see p. 43) that Johnson had deceived Congress by failing to reveal that the *Maddox* had provoked the incident by patrolling inside North Vietnamese territorial waters.

Defoliated: stripped of its leaves by chemicals, in order to make it easier to root out Vietcong guerillas.

During the Tet offensive, 30 South Vietnamese cities and the gardens of the US embassy in Saigon were temporarily occupied by the Vietcong.

Two new terms were introduced into the American vocabulary – 'hawks' and 'doves'. Hawks wanted to continue the war until its objectives were achieved, whatever the cost. Doves argued that the human cost of the war was worth peace at any price.

The death toll among Americans was: 9,378 in 1967 and 14,592 in 1968.

In July 1963 a partial test ban treaty was finally signed, outlawing the testing of new weapons in water or in the atmosphere. But the treaty did not ban underground testing, nor was it signed by France and China, two new nuclear powers. It did nothing to reduce existing stockpiles and was regarded only as a first step. For the rest of the decade, although both sides steered clear of any further direct confrontation, American involvement in Vietnam and the change of leadership in the Soviet Union impeded any more real progress towards easing tensions. Whether this would have been any different had Kennedy lived remains debatable.

The Vietnam quagmire

By 1963 the government of Ngo Dinh Diem in South Vietnam, to whose defence America had been committed since 1954, was under threat from Communist guerillas, the Vietcong, who were aided and supplied by the Communist North. Diem's regime was corrupt and unpopular and could scarcely be called democratic. At first Kennedy rejected his generals' advice to send American troops there, arguing that by forcibly upholding an unpopular government the United States would not only lose the trust of the local population, but might even help to drive them into the arms of the Communists. In the end, however, the domino theory won through, and Kennedy sent a 100,000-strong counter-insurgency force, the Green Berets, opening the way to the fatal US military entanglement in South Vietnam.

This policy of limited involvement did not succeed in crushing the Vietcong, and Kennedy's successor was faced with a choice between withdrawal or escalation. When a US destroyer, the *Maddox*, was torpedoed off the North Vietnamese coast Johnson took advantage of the wave of indignation that swept the country to rush through Congress the Gulf of Tonkin resolution, empowering the President to 'take all necessary measures to repel any armed attack against the forces of the United States and to prevent further armed aggression' – in other words, permission for America to go to war against the Vietcong and the North Vietnamese. Armed with these powers, Johnson set about doing what he had already decided must be done. By the end of 1965, over 200,000 American soldiers were fighting in South Vietnam and Operation Rolling Thunder was bombing the towns and factories of the North to cut off supplies coming to the Vietcong from North Vietnam.

By the end of 1968 there were half a million American servicemen in Vietnam, but victory was nowhere near. Three million tons of bombs had been dropped on the North, numerous Southern villages destroyed, the jungle defoliated and millions of South Vietnamese civilians killed, maimed or made homeless – all to no avail. After three years of such treatment the Vietcong demonstrated that their strength was unbroken when they launched the Tet offensive in February 1968. In addition, atrocities turned uncounted thousands of South Vietnamese peasants against the Americans, thus defeating the whole point of the war.

A minority of Americans had opposed the war from the beginning, but many more, who had at first accepted the Government's arguments that the war was necessary if communism were not to spread all over South-East Asia, turned against it as its effects were brought home to them. Film of the fighting and the atrocities that went with it were shown every night on the television news, and Americans watched with horror and incredulity as villages were destroyed in order to 'save' them. The draft brought home the reality of the war to many young people. Veterans returned home physically or mentally shattered. By 1968 there were few American families whose lives had not been touched by this war, the most unpopular in America's history.

Source A

Policy statement by Robert McNamara, Secretary for Defence, March 1964.

The United States has no designs whatever on the resources and territory of that area [South Vietnam] . . . . Our concern is threefold.

First, and most important, is the simple fact that South Vietnam, a member of the Free World, is striving to preserve its independence from Communist attack. The Vietnamese have asked our help. We have given it. We shall continue to give it.

We do so in their interest . . . . It is not right . . . nor is it in our nature – to abandon them when the going is difficult.

Second, South-East Asia has great significance in the foward defence of the United States . . . . In Communist hands this area would pose a most serious threat to the security of the US and to the family of free-world nations to which we belong. To defend South-East Asia, we must meet the challenge of Vietnam.

And third we must prove in the Vietnamese test case that the free world can cope successfully with Communist wars of liberation as we have coped successfully with Communist aggression at other levels.

Our goal is peace and stability . . . . But we have learned that 'peace at any price' is not practical in the long run, and that the cost of defending freedom must be borne if we are to have it at all.

Source B

From a memorandum to President Johnson from Robert McNamara, Secretary for Defence, 19 May 1967. Soon after this Johnson sacked McNamara and replaced him with Clark Clifford. Once a hawk himself, Clifford soon began to question the usefulness and morality of the war.

There may be a limit beyond which many Americans and much of the world will not permit the United States to go. The picture of the world's greatest superpower killing or seriously injuring 1000 non-combatants a week, while trying to pound a tiny backward nation into submission on an issue whose merits are hotly disputed, is not a pretty one. It could conceivably produce a costly distortion . . . in the world image of the United States – especially if the damage to North Vietnam is complete enough to be 'successful'.

An anti-Vietnam demonstration in Washington DC. In time, the war became the most unpopular in American history.

It must not be forgotten that Communist China, which was implacably hostile to the USA was now also a great power, having successfully exploded her first atomic bomb in 1964.

? ?

1 Examine the case made in source A for US involvement in South Vietnam. Are these the arguments you would expect from an American politician of the 1960s? Explain your answer.

2 How have McNamara's priorities, as expressed in source B, altered by 1967? Is he likely to have changed his mind again by the end of 1968?

3 In the face of all this, why should President Johnson have insisted on continuing the war?

Conclusion

Abroad, as at home, the 1960s began in optimism and ended in turmoil. The Cuban crisis alerted the Superpowers to the danger of nuclear war, and for a while it seemed as though the end of the Cold War was in sight. With hindsight, it seems unlikely that this would have happened even if Kennedy had lived, for the underlying conflicts of interest between the United States and the Soviet Union remained unsolved. The unwinnable war in Vietnam, for example, was not just Johnson's personal policy but the logical result of 20 years of Containment, a policy accepted by all Presidents, including Kennedy. And to the American nightmare in South-East Asia no end was yet in sight, as the Nixon administration began its five-year search for a way to withdraw without admitting defeat.

6 CRISES OLD AND NEW: THE USA AT HOME IN THE 1970S

The Chicago Eight were anti-war activists charged with crossing state lines to start a riot at the 1968 Democratic Convention. Tom Hayden was one of the defendants.

Angela Davis was a black Communist accused of taking part in an attempt to free a group of black prisoners during their trial in 1970, which resulted in the deaths of four people. Her trial in San José in 1972 attracted worldwide attention. The jury aquitted her.

Presidents:
Richard M. Nixon 1968-74
Gerald R. Ford 1974-6
Jimmy Carter 1976-80

President Nixon inherited an angry and divided nation. During his first term in office social unrest reached its peak with the demonstrations against the invasion of Cambodia (Kampuchea) in May 1970, during which four students were shot dead by National Guardsmen at Kent State University in Ohio, and the trials of the Chicago Eight in 1969 and Angela Davis in 1972.

After this, the wave of dissent gradually subsided and society did not fall apart. The backlash against many of the social and political changes of the 1960s gathered momentum. The Nixon government reflected this new mood – with its slow-down on civil rights, withdrawal of federal support for busing schemes (see p. 40), and appointment of more conservative judges to the Supreme Court. Nixon was re-elected in 1972 with a resounding majority

The idols of the silent majority: Richard M. Nixon and Spiro T. Agnew celebrate their selection as the Republican team for the 1968 presidential elections. They promised to restore law and order and traditional values, as well as bringing American troops home from Vietnam.

over the liberal Democrat George McGovern, whom the Republicans denounced as the champion of 'acid [LSD], abortion and amnesty [for draft-dodgers]'. Nixon was forced to resign in 1974 due to the Watergate scandal. His place was taken by Vice-President Gerald Ford, who was defeated in 1976 by Democrat Jimmy Carter from Georgia.

Race, poverty and the inner cities

In spite of everything, Blacks had made much progress in the 1960s. A sizeable black middle class emerged and senior black elected officials became commonplace, even in Southern cities. During the early 1970s the last vestiges of legal segregation disappeared from the South, and many Blacks benefited from the anti-poverty programmes that halved the number of very poor Americans.

Many Blacks, however, were still left behind. Unemployment among Blacks in 1980 was twice that of Whites, among black teenagers four times as much. According to the 1973 census, 24.5 million Americans still lived below the official poverty line of $4732 for a family of four, and much of this poverty was concentrated among Blacks and Hispanics in the inner cities, where the cycle of deprivation, which began with poor schools, was still only too apparent. The cities themselves were depressing places in which to live, with high rates of violent crime made worse by the lax US gun-control laws.

It was not enough, it was argued, just to dismantle the apparatus of segregation and provide equality of education on paper. Disadvantaged groups must be helped to make the most of their new opportunities through programmes of 'positive discrimination' or 'affirmative action'. Employers were ordered to reserve a fixed quota of jobs for ethnic minorities in proportion to their numbers in the community and colleges to regulate the admission of students, especially on popular courses like medicine, in the same way. In order to achieve racially and socially balanced schools, and thus eliminate the differences in quality between inner city and suburban schools, courts ordered education authorities to 'bus' selected children out of their own neighbourhoods to schools in other areas, a measure that became an emotive issue in American politics.

The entry of Blacks into the mainstream of political life continued throughout the 1970s, so that by the mid-1980s Washington DC, Chicago, Los Angeles, Philadelphia, Detroit, Atlanta, Birmingham (Alabama), Newark and Spokane (Washington) all had or had had black mayors. In 1984 the Revd Jesse Jackson ran for the Democratic presidential nomination against Walter Mondale (see p. 55).

Hispanics: Spanish-speaking Americans of Latin American descent.

For a taste of the racial mix of the American inner city of the 1970s and 1980s see the television series 'Hill Street Blues'.

The inner city. A scene from New York's Lower East Side.

Source A

From the Supreme Court judgement in the case of Green v. County School Board of New Kent County, Virginia, May 1968. When ordered to desegregate in the early 1960s the district had done so by opening its schools to everyone on a free-for-all basis. A local parent had taken the school board to court on the grounds that the freedom of choice was largely illusory and did not constitute real desegregation.

Source B

From the Supreme Court ruling in the case of Swann v. Charlotte-Mecklenburg Board of Education, North Carolina, April 1971. A local parent brought a legal action claiming that the school district's own plans for redrawing the catchment area and busing pupils were not radical enough to bring about real differences in the racial composition of schools.

Source C

From President Nixon's address to the nation on Equal Educational Opportunity and School Busing, 16 March 1972.

Moratorium: legally authorized postponement of an activity.

A 'freedom of choice' plan, which allows a pupil to choose his own public [state] school . . . cannot be accepted as a sufficient step to effectuate a transition to a unitary, non-racial system, where, in three years of operation of the plan, not a single white child has chosen to attend a Negro school, and, although a number of Negro children have enrolled in the white school, 85 per cent of the Negro children in the system still attend the Negro school.

'Racially neutral' assignment plans proposed by school authorities may be inadequate; such plans may fail to counteract the continuing effects of segregated residence patterns . . . . In these cases affirmative action in the form of remedial altering of attendance zones is proper to achieve truly non-discriminatory assignments . . . and this court recognizes the importance of bus transportation as a normal and accepted tool of educational policy in this respect . . . . These remedies may be administratively awkward, inconvenient, and even bizarre in some situations and may impose burdens on some; but all awkwardness and inconvenience cannot be avoided in the interim period when remedial adjustments are being made to eliminate segregated school systems.

My own position is well-known. I am opposed to busing for the purpose of achieving racial balance in our schools . . . . And I believe most Americans, white and black, share that view . . .

The purpose of such busing is to help end segregation. But experience in case after case has shown that busing is a bad means to a good end.

But what we need now is not just speaking out against more busing. We need action to stop it. Above all, we need action to stop it in the right way – in a way that will provide better education for every child in America in a desegregated school system . . . .

The decisions [by the courts] have left in their wake . . . anger, fear and turmoil in local communities; and, worst of all, agonized concern among hundreds of thousands of parents for the education and safety of their children who have been forced by court order to be bused miles away from their neighbourhood schools . . . .

That is why I am sending a special message to Congress tomorrow urging immediate consideration and action on two measures. First, I shall propose legislation that would call an immediate halt to all new busing orders by federal courts – a moratorium of new busing. Next, I shall propose a companion measure – the Equal Educational Opportunities Act of 1972. This act would require that every state or locality grant equal educational opportunity to every person, regardless of race, color or national origin . . . . The act I propose would concentrate federal school funds on the areas of greatest educational need . . . . It is time for us to make a national commitment to see that the schools in the central cities are upgraded so that the children who go there will have just as good a chance to get quality education as do children who go to school in the suburbs.

? ?

1 What does the supreme Court mean by a 'freedom of choice' plan and a 'racially neutral' plan? Why does the court consider that these will not produce equality of opportunity for all children in the area? What suggestion does it offer instead in source B?.

2 What are President Nixon's objections to busing? What kind of Americans may he be speaking on behalf of?

3 What alternative suggestion for equal opportunity does Nixon put forward? On what grounds might a supporter of busing argue that Nixon's ideas will not bring about equal opportunity for underprivileged children?

Anti-busing riots in Boston. White youths throw stones at the police during a demonstration at the South Boston High School. President Nixon's opposition to compulsory busing helped him to be re-elected in 1972.

tax base: personal wealth, in the form of income and property, which the city government can tax to finance its services.

Automobile production fell during the 1970s from 13 million vehicles a year to 7 million.

Some of the songs of Bruce Springsteen deal with this aspect of urban decay (see especially, 'My Hometown').

Nixon's opposition to busing was matched by protests from anti-busing parents all over the cities of the North. By the end of the 1970s, some districts, including, ironically, Charlotte-Mecklenburg, had successfully integrated their schools and come as close as possible to providing equality of opportunity. Many other areas, however, including New York, Los Angeles and Detroit, scaled down or abandoned their busing schemes, and their schools remained divided into poor-quality, mainly black inner city ones and those of the affluent, predominently white suburbs. Some professionally successful Blacks managed to escape the cycle by moving to the suburbs themselves; many more remained trapped in the deprivation of the inner cities.

A new twist to the urban crisis emerged in the mid-1970s. As the affluent abandoned the inner cities, their tax bases shrank, while the demand for services continued to grow. Most major cities experienced difficulties in balancing their books, and in 1975 New York only narrowly avoided having to declare itself bankrupt.

Another urban problem developed with the further decline, in the face of foreign competition and worldwide overproduction, of heavy industries like steel, automobiles and textiles. As plants closed, whole towns like Youngstown (Ohio), Homestead (Pennsylvania) and Detroit were thrown into depression – shops closed, homes were repossessed by mortgage companies and local services were run down, creating a new class of urban poor.

Minorities

The 1960s and the black rebellion left their mark in the raised consciousness of minorities who, suddenly aware of how their interests had been suppressed in the past, began to demand their rights. Most widespread was the Women's Liberation Movement, which pressurized Congress into passing the Equal Rights Amendment (ERA) in 1972 and 17 states into legalizing abortion.

The results were mixed. By 1980 there was a great increase in the number of women working outside the home and there were more women in high positions, including a justice of the Supreme Court, Sandra Day O'Connor, and a handful of female state governors and big city mayors. Most women, however, continued to work in the traditional, low-paid 'women's' jobs like typing and nursing – the so-called 'female ghetto'. The ERA was never ratified by the states and lapsed in 1982. On the other hand, social attitudes began to change. Women in general became more self-reliant and less ready to tolerate bad treatment or unsatisfactory marriages. The number of women voluntarily bringing up children on their own rose steadily.

Inspired by the Black Power slogan, other minority groups questioned the assumption that to get on in American society you had to integrate completely and reject your own cultural heritage. Spanish-speaking Americans demanded bilingual education. Homosexuals, renaming themselves 'gays', came out into the open and fought discrimination. Native Americans, long a forgotten minority living on remote reservations, argued for the wrongs done to them in the last century to be put right. This came to the world's attention in 1973, when a group of Sioux occupied the town of Wounded Knee in South Dakota, scene of a massacre in 1890, and held out against a force of Federal Marshals and FBI agents for 71 days.

Women's Liberation began in earnest in 1963 with the publication of *The Feminine Mystique* by Betty Frieden, who argued that women could not find fulfilment by living through their husbands and children, but only through achievement in their own right.

As the ERA was a constitutional amendment, it required the formal approval of two-thirds of the states before it became law.

In 1969 Indians occupied Alcatraz Island in San Francisco Bay, once a high-security prison, as a protest against the white man's pollution of the environment. In Washington State, Indians organized 'fish-ins' on rivers where Indians had traditionally fished which were now closed to them.

For the 1890 massacre, see Dee Brown, *Bury my Heart at Wounded Knee*, 1971.

Red Power! 500 Native Americans occupy the offices of the Bureau of Indian Affairs in Washington in November 1972. They said they would remain there until Indian land rights, stolen from them in the broken treaties of the nineteenth century, were restored.

Source A
Testimony of Evan Harney, an Oklahoman Indian, before a Senate Committee, 1973. In the 1970s American westerns were, in fact, beginning to change. Whereas the traditional western showed the Indian as the villain, films of

I have grown up with racism all my life. When I was a child, watching cowboys and Indians on TV, I would root for the cavalry, not the Indians. It was that bad. I was that far towards my own destruction . . .

Though 50 per cent of the children at the country school I attended in Oklahoma were Indians, nothing in school, on television, or on the radio taught anything about Indian culture. There were no books on Indian history, not even in the library . . .

the 1970s were more sympathetic to the Indian cause (see especially *Little Big Man*, starring Dustin Hoffman, which has been shown on British television).

Source B

From an article in *Newsweek*, 6 June 1977.

Dade County is the county in which Miami is situated.

The Dade County ordinance was, in fact, rejected in the referendum, and Republican Koch's (the future Mayor Koch of New York) bill did not pass Congress.

But I knew something was wrong. I started reading and learning my own culture.

I saw the Indian people at their happiest when they went to Alcatraz or to Washington to defend their fishing rights. They at last felt like human beings.

All over Miami, sexual fundamentalists and gay activists are mobilizing for a somewhat bizarre but deadly serious battle over gay rights. The contest is led by two unlikely adversaries: singer, Anita Bryant . . . and Jack Campbell, 44, owner of a nationwide chain of 40 gay bathhouses. The immediate issue is next week's referendum on a Dade County ordinance that bans discrimination in employment and housing based on a person's 'affectional or sexual preference'.

To many of the nation's 20 million homosexuals, the vote – the first of its kind in a major city – is a crucial test of whether the country is willing to extend civil rights legislation to homosexuals . . . . For her part, Bryant vows that if she succeeds in overturning the local anti-discrimination ordinance, she will go national with her God and decency crusade. If she wins, there is little chance that a Congressional anti-discrimination bill, sponsored by Rep. Edward Koch of New York, will pass any time soon.

??

1 In what different ways do gays and Indians feel that they have been discriminated against in the past? What effect might this have had on them as individuals?

2 Why is it now, in the 1970s, that they are becoming more assertive and what sort of demands are they making?

3 What indications are there in source B of the sort of obstacles minorities might encounter? Do you know of any minority groups today that are demanding greater rights? What sort of arguments do people put up against them?

Watergate and the crisis of the American political system

It seems likely that the background to this incident must be looked for in Nixon's own character. He was suspicious by nature and sensitive to criticism, taking incidents such as the Cambodia riots (see p. 38) and Congress' refusal to pass some of his programmes as personal affronts. This mood was aggravated early in 1972, when opinion polls revealed a Democratic lead in the run-up to the elections. According to observers, he became almost paranoid, convinced that he was surrounded by enemies.

On the night of 17 June 1972 five men were caught red-handed fitting electronic bugging devices in Democratic Party Headquarters in the Watergate building in Washington. It soon came to light that they were members of CREEP, the Committee to Re-Elect the President (in the November 1972 elections), which was headed by Nixon's friend and former Attorney-General, John Mitchell. At the time, Nixon was able to brush off the incident as a case of over-enthusiastic employees overstepping the mark. The bugging made little impact on the public and Nixon went on to win the election.

However, at the CREEP members' trial in January 1973 Judge Sirica voiced doubts that the full story was being told, and in the months that followed two *Washington Post* reporters, Carl Bernstein and Bob Woodward, unearthed evidence that high-up officials in the Nixon government, perhaps even the President himself, had authorized the break-in and then tried to cover up their involvement. The Senate set up an investigating committee under Senator Sam Ervin.

The committee turned over a can of worms that damaged not only Nixon's reputation but that of past Presidents as well. Johnson's deceit over the Gulf of Tonkin incident (see p. 36) had already come to light in 1971, when the *New York Times* had published the 'Pentagon Papers', information about the inner workings of the Johnson administration leaked to it by a former Pentagon official, Daniel Ellsberg. Now it was revealed that Nixon had committed many illegal acts, encroaching on the civil liberties of individuals and ignoring the

Along the way, it also came to light that Vice-President Spiro T. Agnew had taken bribes and fiddled his tax returns. He was forced to resign in 1973 and was replaced by Gerald Ford.

A left-wing government, headed by Salvador Allende had been elected in 1970 and was overthrown in 1973 by a CIA-backed coup by army officers under General Pinochet, who retains the support of the USA today.

The interests of 'national security' were often used by Presidents as a justification for illegal acts.

James McCord, one of the convicted Watergate burglars, testifying before the Senate Investigating Committee in May 1973. He is holding up one of the bugging devices that were used on phones in the Democratic Party headquarters in June 1972.

Impeachment: the power given to Congress by the US constitution to sack a corrupt or incompetent President. It has only been used once before, in an unsuccessful attempt to remove President Andrew Johnson in 1868.

rule that no President was above the law. He had burgled the office of Ellsberg's psychiatrist in the hope that the Pentagon Papers would seem less damning if the man who had leaked them could be proved to be mentally or emotionally unstable. He had authorized phone-tapping, attacked neutral Cambodia without Congressional consent, lied to the press, allowed the CIA to meddle in Chilean affairs and evaded income tax. Another Senate committee, the Church Committee, investigated the past activities of the FBI and CIA. It revealed in 1975 that even Roosevelt and Kennedy, two of the most admired Presidents of the twentieth century, allowed the FBI to tap the phones and open the mail of political opponents who had done nothing illegal, and that CIA agents had attempted to assassinate important foreign leaders, including Castro of Cuba, Lumumba of the Congo (Zaïre) and Diem of South Vietnam.

The Ervin Committee also discovered that Nixon routinely recorded all his conversations on tape. For over a year he refused to hand over the tapes, although he was legally obliged to do so. By the time he finally gave in, it no longer mattered that the evidence revealed was not quite sufficient to convict him beyond all reasonable doubt of actually authorizing the Watergate break-in. Eighteen months of evasion and lying, plus mounting evidence of illegal acts stretching back to 1968 had been enough to turn even his own Republican party against him. Threatened with impeachment, Nixon resigned on 9 August 1974 and was automatically succeeded by Gerald Ford.

In the 1976 election Ford was defeated by Jimmy Carter from Georgia, whom few people had heard of before that year. He posed as an honest man, free from the corruption of Nixon's Washington and told Americans, 'I'll never lie to you'.

Source A
From the Articles of Impeachment issued by the House of Representatives Judiciary Committee, 4 August 1974.

Article I
In his conduct of the office of President of the United States, Richard M. Nixon, in violation of his constitutional oath faithfully to execute the office of President of the United States . . . and in violation of his constitutional duty to take care that the laws be faithfully executed, has prevented, obstructed and impeded the administration of justice . . . . Richard M. Nixon, using the powers of his high office, engaged personally and through his subordinates and agents in a course of conduct or plan designed to delay, impede and obstruct the investigation of such unlawful entry, to cover-up, conceal and protect those responsible . . . .

Article II
Using the power of the office of President of the United States, Richard M. Nixon has repeatedly engaged in conduct violating the constitutional rights of citizens.

Source B
From an article by an American historian, Henry Steele Commager, in a special issue of *Time*, 19 August 1974, covering Nixon's resignation and its implications.

The Watergate affair has been a tragedy but not an unmitigated disaster for the American people, for we have learned much from it; we can almost say we have profited from it . . . . Without disorder or even excessive bitterness, we have removed Mr Nixon and quietly installed Mr Ford. This is a revolution. In most countries of the globe it would be a violent revolution, but in the US it is peaceful and legal . . . .

Some questions that should have been settled remain, to be sure, unsettled. The question of presidential war-making . . . or the balance (if any) between the claims of national security and the guarantees of the Bill of Rights . . . but it is highly probable that for all practical purposes they have been answered by public opinion. It is wildly improbable that President Ford or his successors in the foreseeable future will wage war on a neutral country . . . interfere with the processes of justice, openly flout the guarantees of freedom of speech and the press or seek to establish a police state – all of which Mr Nixon did.

? ?

1 What are the accusations levelled at Nixon in Articles I and II of Source A, and what specific incidents do the authors have in mind?

2 What misdeeds does Commager lay at Nixon's door in source B? What specific events does he have in mind?

3 On what grounds does Commager argue:
a good may come out of this crisis?
b Americans have reason to be proud as well as ashamed of the way the Watergate crisis worked out?
Has his optimism been justified by events since then? Think about this last question as you read the rest of this book.

The energy crisis

Since 1945 Americans had assumed that their's was a society of unlimited abundance. But in the 1970s the myth of the ever-expanding economy was rudely shattered.

The decade began with inflation, which had been triggered off by the Vietnam War. Prices in 1970 were 16 per cent higher than in 1967 and still rising. The value of the dollar on the foreign exchange markets began to drop. The biggest shock came in October 1973 when OPEC quadrupled the price of oil and banned its export to the United States and Western Europe in the aftermath of the Yom Kippur War. America's economic growth had depended on cheap energy, and her way of life on the automobile. Overnight the petrol pumps ran dry and factories were threatened with closure. Higher oil prices fuelled inflation, and government attempts to curb it brought recession and the highest unemployment rate since the 1930s. With the cost of imports exceeding that of exports, the federal budget went into the red. No one knew what to do about the combined problem of inflation and stagnation – 'stagflation', as it was nicknamed. President Carter's energy-saving programme, which he called the 'moral equivalent of war', proved ineffective.

The oil shortages proved short-lived (there was another one in 1979 following the fall of the Shah of Iran) but energy prices remained high and the economic problems of the 1970s had a profound effect on American society. Groups that had climbed out of poverty in the 1960s were thrust back down

OPEC – Organization of Petroleum Exporting Countries – is an association of oil-producing states with an Arab majority, who have agreed to act together to control the output and price of oil, so that their economies will benefit more. The 1973 protest was against Western support for Israel in the war of October 1973.

8.5 million, or 9 per cent of the working population.

It made so little impact that Carter's critics, noticing the initials, nicknamed it 'meow'.

Protest against petrol shortages turned to violence in many parts of the USA. Here in Levittown, Pennsylvania, in June 1979, cars were set on fire by angry demonstrators.

The gap between black and white incomes, which had narrowed in the 1960s, widened again.

One of the most noticeable and permanent effects of the energy crisis was the disappearance from American roads of the 'gas guzzlers' of the 1950s and 1960s – to be replaced by smaller, European-style cars. Another outcome was the imposition of a blanket 55 m.p.h. speed limit on all roads, which is still in force today.

It is hard to recall that as late as the early 1960s jeans were the uniform of a tiny, rebellious minority, and that few women would dare be seen on the streets in trousers.

As compared with between 70 and 80 per cent in the average British general election. Reagan gained 50.8 per cent of the votes actually cast in 1980 and therefore won only 27 per cent of the possible vote.

again by mounting inflation. Unemployment created new pockets of urban deprivation. As important were the psychological effects. As people felt less economically secure and less optimistic about the future, they became more self-interested and less concerned with the fate of the poor and underprivileged. In the aftermath of inflation and shortages, the last of the 1960s idealism died out.

At the same time, the energy crisis also opened a debate on the whole morality of the American consumer society, which ate up vast quantities of the world's non-renewable resources and polluted the environment. The words 'ecology' and 'conservation' entered into the everyday vocabulary. The pros and cons of nuclear energy became a subject of public debate in 1979 when a serious accident took place at the nuclear power station at Three Mile Island near Harrisburg in Pennsylvania.

Conclusion

The 1970s was a decade of contradictions. In some ways the spirit of the 1960s lived on. Minorities asserted themselves. Changes in dress, language and behaviour were permanently incorporated into American life. On the other hand, a swing back to more traditional values had begun, and an attack opened on the 1960s fashions in sexual behaviour, drug-taking, child-centred education and abortion. While minorities succeeded in bringing about some changes in attitudes, their achievements often fell far short of their goals and provoked a backlash among more conventional members of the population. And, while Blacks entered the mainstream of American politics and race declined as an issue, the problem of the black and Hispanic underclass trapped in the inner cities was not solved.

Two great and unexpected crises shook the nation. The United States survived the Watergate scandal with its democracy intact, but Watergate, the Pentagon Papers and the revelations of the Church Committee shook people's faith in the politicians. In the 1980 election only about 50 per cent of those eligible to vote actually did so. And the politics of the 1980s were to be greatly influenced by the shockwaves of the economic troubles of the 1970s, which burst upon Americans after two and a half decades of unparalleled prosperity.

7 THE DEATH OF OLD CERTAINTIES: THE USA AND THE WORLD IN THE 1970S

Although Nixon had made his reputation as a fire-eating anti-Communist, as President he was forced to face the ever-present risk of nuclear confrontation that went with East-West hostility. This problem was made more acute by the rise to Superpower status of China, with whom US relations had been bad since 1949. In Vietnam no easy answer was in sight. Nixon had promised to 'bring the boys home' but was determined to do it without loss of face.

Detente

The arms race continued throughout the 1960s, putting great strain on the American economy. With China now in the race, the expense and danger could only get worse. In these circumstances, Nixon did a surprising about-face and, with his foreign policy adviser, Henry Kissinger, devised the policy of Detente, which was continued until 1979 by his successor, Jimmy Carter. The USA and the Soviet Union tried to reduce tension in small and practical ways. Visits were exchanged. A treaty was signed defining the status of Berlin. The 1975 Helsinki Security Conference finalized Europe's post-1945 borders. Trade was encouraged and surplus American grain sold cheaply to Russia in years when the harvest was poor. A Strategic Arms Limitation Treaty (SALT I) was signed in 1972. No reduction in existing armaments was involved, but limitations were imposed on the future construction of ICBMs. Further talks – SALT II – continued throughout the 1970s.

The most dramatic breakthrough came in relations with China. The world was taken by surprise in 1971, when an American table-tennis team was

Nixon visited Moscow in 1972. Brezhnev visited Washington the following year.

America had never recognized the post-1945 Polish frontiers. The Soviet Union had never recognized the existence of West Germany. Neither of the two German Republics recognized the right of the other to exist. In 1975 (and in a series of treaties between the Soviet Union and European nations) many of these outstanding issues were settled.

The great diplomatic about-face. President Nixon at the home of Chairman Mao Zedong in Peking, February 1972.

The process of improving relations with China was dubbed by the press 'ping-pong diplomacy'.

These events were only made possible by corresponding changes in Chinese attitudes to the west, which were caused by her quarrel with Russia in the 1960s.

From the introduction to a book written by Harriman in 1975 about his experiences as a special envoy to Stalin and Churchill between 1941 and 1946.

In 1971 the bombing of North Vietnam was also resumed. Altogether, in the process of withdrawal, Nixon dropped more bombs on the North than Johnson had done.

There was no suggestion this time of direct American military intervention. For a view of the fall of Kampuchea, see the film *The Killing Fields*.

invited to play in Beijing. After that, events moved quickly. President Nixon visited China in 1972 and dropped US opposition to Communist China taking up the Chinese seat on the United Nations Security Council. At the same time a slow chipping away at the American commitment to the defence of Taiwan began (see p. 11).

Detente was a step on the road to Kennedy's world made 'safe for diversity', and the long-running debate over the wisdom of making agreements with the Russians revived. Opinion was divided, once again, between those who argued that all Communists, Russian or Chinese, were mortal enemies dedicated to eradicating democracy from the earth, who signed agreements with the West only to hide their true intentions; and those like former US ambassador to Moscow, Averell Harriman, who wrote in 1975:

I continue to maintain that on ideology there is no prospect of compromise between the Kremlin and ourselves, but that we must find ways to settle as many areas of conflict as possible in order to live together on this small planet without war . . . . It seems to me that we have no choice.

The end of Containment

Nixon's answer to the problem of withdrawal from Vietnam was 'Vietnamization' – the equipping and training of the south Vietnamese army to the point where it became capable of defending the country itself. To buy the time needed to get this project off the ground, the neighbouring neutral state of Cambodia (Kampuchea), which the Vietcong used as a base, was first bombed (something that was kept secret from Congress) and then invaded in March 1970, triggering off anti-war demonstrations on American university campuses and a bitter debate in Congress over the President's duplicity.

In January 1973 a ceasefire was finally signed, which hid an American withdrawal behind a cloak of respectability. Both Vietnams promised that they would not again seek a military solution to their differences. All US ground troops were then withdrawn. Whether the ceasefire would hold depended solely on the good faith of both sides.

In March 1975, North Vietnam invaded the South and the Southern army crumbled. When President Ford asked Congress for $422 million to help the South Vietnamese, it was refused. Within a month South Vietnam and Cambodia had fallen to the Communists, bringing about the very result that ten years of US involvement had been designed to prevent.

The End! An American helicopter evacuating American and foreign nationals from Saigon as the Communists move in, April, 1975.

Source A
From an article in *Time*, 14 April 1975.

Though Americans were saddened by the collapse of Indo-China, US congressmen touring their districts during the Easter recess encountered practically no support for President Ford's plea for further military aid. Observed Democrat Don Bunker of Washington State: 'People are drained. They want to bury the memory of Indo-China. They regard it as a tragic chapter in American life, but they want no further part of it . . . .' Typical of voter reaction that congressmen heard was the angry observation of Dan Merwin, a fireman in Girard, Ohio: 'They're going down the drain without a fight, and we're still talking of sending them hundreds of millions of dollars! I don't understand it. We've got people starving in West Virginia.'

Source B
A letter to *Time*, 14 April 1975.

4 July 1976 was the two hundredth anniversary of the signing of the Declaration of Independence, which is regarded as the birthday of the USA. 1976 was celebrated as the bicentennial year.

Where is the spirit of '76? During this Bicentennial of our hard-won freedom, we are searching for ways to celebrate while we stand by and watch first Cambodia, then South Vietnam fall to an aggressor . . . . As the dominoes fall, will it be Thailand next, then South Korea and so on? These people have fought and are still fighting for the same basic reasons for which we took on Great Britain.

Are we to celebrate with fireworks while rockets are crushing freedom in other parts of the world? What a time for us to deserve a Congress like this.

? ?

1 For what reasons, both practical and emotional, does the writer in source B think that the Americans owe the non-Communists of South-East Asia their support?

2 Why, according to source A, are so many Americans in 1975 so unwilling to give even financial aid to Vietnam? What developments inside the USA might be contributing to this reaction?

3 Do you think the last sentence in source B is a fair comment?

President Carter and human rights

By 1976 most Americans had no stomach left for the policy of Containment but there was no consensus on what should replace it. In his inaugural speech in January 1977, however, President Carter announced that henceforth the United States would follow a clear policy of respect for human rights:

Quoted in *Newsweek*, 15 March 1977.

Because we are free we can never be indifferent to the fate of freedom elsewhere. Our moral sense dictates a clearcut preference for those societies which share with us an abiding respect for individual human rights.

Critics argued that this policy was impractical. It would offend allies like Iran, Chile and South Korea – all of whom were guilty of gross human rights violations at home – and thereby weaken American security. Criticism of the Soviet Union's human rights record would wreck Detente. 'Bukovsky [a Soviet dissident whose case was taken up by Carter]', wrote an English diplomat in horror, 'is not worth the world'.

One Senator argued against the treaty on the grounds that 'we stole it fair and square'.

Carter had some successes. He forced through Congress a treaty giving the Panama Canal, which had been acquired by the USA by deceit in 1904, back to Panama. He gave his blessing to the left-wing Sandanista regime that seized power from the corrupt dictatorship of General Somoza in Nicaragua in 1979. He backed the British scheme to resolve the long-standing South Rhodesian crisis, which resulted in the independent Black African state of Zimbabwe being set up in 1980. His encouragement for the efforts of President Sadat of Egypt and Prime Minister Begin of Israel to make peace between their countries resulted in the Camp David accords of 1978.

A peace treaty was signed between the two nations after 30 years of emnity, and Israel agreed to give back the Sinai Desert, seized in 1967.

As predicted, Carter paid a heavy price for his expressions of sympathy with

President Carter's (centre) moment of triumph. With Prime Minister Begin of Israel and President Sadat of Egypt he celebrates the success of the Camp David talks in September 1978. In spite of a number of achievements, Carter's foreign policy ended in humiliation and paved the way for the election of Ronald Reagan in 1980.

Soviet dissidents, when the Soviet Union refused to sign SALT II until 1979. When the Russians invaded Afghanistan in December 1979 Carter reacted with horror. He refused to ratify SALT II, which the Russians had just finally signed, increased defence expenditure, placed an embargo on further grain sales and withdrew American athletes from the 1980 Moscow Olympics. By mid-1980 relations between the Superpowers were frostier than they had been for years.

The Iranian hostage crisis

For 20 years, the United States had backed the Shah as a bulwark against the spread of communism in the Middle East and the protector of American oil supplies. In 1977 the Shah hinted that if the United States made arms supplies dependent on an improved civil rights record in Iran, he might buy weapons from the Russians instead. This apparently scared Carter back into line.

National Security Adviser, Zbigniew Brzezinski, favoured continued and increased support for the Shah to help him stay in power.

Theocratic regime: government by the priesthood.

In the case of Iran, Carter allowed his concern for human rights to take second place to America's need for the Shah's friendship. Throughout the Carter era the United States continued to supply Iran with arms, even though many of these found their way into the hands of Savak, the secret police, and were used to suppress internal opposition. Here Carter not only contravened his principles but made a gross error of judgment.

In January 1979 the Shah was ousted by a popular revolution and replaced by a theocratic regime under the Muslim holy man, the Ayatollah Khomeini, who was bitterly hostile to the United States. When Carter allowed the exiled Shah to enter America for medical treatment in October, Iranian students seized the American embassy in Teheran and held 50 Americans hostage for 444 days. A rescue attempt by United States' commandos in April 1980 was a dismal failure. The hostages were finally released minutes after President Reagan had been inaugurated, a deliberate slap in the face for Carter.

Source A
From a letter to *Time*, 24 December 1979. For years the United States had supported unpopular and undemocratic governments in the Philippines and South Korea on the grounds of American strategic interests – the United States had important air and naval bases in both countries.

The explosion of anti-Americanism in Iran may be only the beginning. The Shahs, Somozas, Parks [South Korean leader] and Marcoses [President of the Philippines] of this world have left an angry mob of people who blame the US support of these dictators for years of oppression. The sins of shallow foreign policy are coming back to haunt us all.

Source B
From a letter to *Time*, October 1980.

A reference to *Gulliver's Travels* by Jonathan Swift.

It has now been almost a year since the hostages were seized, and yet Washington still stands by helplessly. America has become a lethargic giant. The Lilliputians have taken to the field with ladders, ropes and pickets to tie down the United States . . . . It is time we had a leader who would take action to end our humiliation. If we do not get one soon, we shall be confined for ever to the ranks of the second-rate powers.

? ?

1 What is the chief difference between the two letter-writers above in their reaction to the Iranian crisis?

2 What answer might President Carter give to the accusations in source B that he has been spineless in his handling of the crisis?

3 If the mood of the second letter-writer is widespread in the United States, what effect might this have on the 1980 election, in which Carter intends to run again?

The hostages return, 19 January 1981, after 444 days of captivity. The incident stung American pride.

Conclusion

The last year of Carter's presidency was a traumatic one. The hostage crisis had revealed that anti-Americanism was rampant in many parts of the world, especially the Islamic ones. Added to this was a feeling of injured pride as it was shown how little the United States, for all her military might, could do to protect her citizens abroad. It was the tragedy of the well-meaning President Carter that he became the personal focus of this anti-Americanism and ended up being despised by his own countrymen as well for being unable to do anything about it.

1980 – the year of 'pure hell' (in Carter's own words) – might have led to a mood of national reappraisal, a serious determination to discover just what had gone wrong with America's relations with the rest of the world and why. In fact, as source B above shows, it triggered off a quite different reaction in the American public, which helped Ronald Reagan win in 1980.

8 THE REAGAN YEARS: 1980~

In 1978 Californians voted for a law linking future rises in property taxes.

The spread of Acquired Immune Deficiency Syndrome (AIDS), which first appeared among the gay communities of New York and San Francisco in 1979, added to the backlash against permissiveness

A number of well-known liberal Senators lost their seats, including George McGovern of South Dakota (see p. 39) and Frank Church of Idaho (see p. 44).

He had been Governor of California 1964-70.

Source A
Extracts from Reagan's acceptance speech for the 1980 Republican nomination, made on 17 July 1980 at the Republican National Convention in Detroit.

President:
Ronald Reagan 1980-

The revolt against the permissiveness and liberalism of the 1960s and 1970s reached a climax in 1980. Taxpayers rebelled against rising welfare costs and argued that too much welfare created a class of shirkers who failed to accept their responsibilities towards their families. Whites and males complained of the unfairness of affirmative action programmes. Communities affected by random violence blamed the courts for being too 'soft' on criminals and demanded the return of the death penalty. Many Americans worried about the effects of the 'permissive society' on family life and about the widespread use of heroin and cocaine. Evangelical, or Fundamentalist, preachers like the Revd Jerry Falwell, who taught a strict moral code based on a literal interpretation of the Bible, used television to gain a mass following. In their relations with the rest of the world Americans felt humiliated and were willing to listen to anyone who promised to restore their pride and status as a great nation.

The triumph of conservatism

Ronald Reagan easily beat Jimmy Carter in 1980 and the Republicans won a majority in both houses of Congress. Most suburbanites voted for Reagan, as did the voters of Middle America, the sunbelt states and all of the Deep South except for Georgia. Only Blacks voted as a block for Carter.

Although he was 70 in 1980, Reagan had considerable charm and was able to convey the impression that he had the answer to society's problems. A former movie actor, he came over well on television, and his speeches sounded convincing even when they had little content. The press dubbed him the 'Great Communicator'. It was not by charm alone, however, that Reagan won the confidence of millions of Americans, for his philosophy and style suited the mood of the nation.

They [the Democrats] say that the United States has had its day in the sun; that our nation has passed its zenith. They expect you to tell your children that the American people no longer have the will to cope with their problems; that the future will be one of sacrifices and few opportunities.

I will not stand by and watch this great country destroy itself under mediocre leadership that drifts from one crisis to the next, eroding our national will and purpose.

Here Reagan explains that one of the main causes of unemployment and the loss of confidence in America's future is the lack of incentive to save and invest that has been brought about by the high rates of taxation needed to finance welfare programmes. He promises to introduce a 30 per cent cut in income tax, spread over three years, and to reduce the welfare budget. This is really the only concrete proposal in this part of the speech.

Work and family are at the center of our lives; the foundation of our dignity as a free people. When we deprive people of what they have earned, or take away their jobs, we destroy their dignity and undermine their families.

These are concepts that stem from the foundation of an economic system that for more than two hundred years has helped us master a continent, create a previously undreamed-of prosperity and had fed millions of others around the globe. That system will continue to serve us in the future if our Government will stop ignoring the basic values on which it was built.

Ronald Reagan campaigning in Florida in 1980.

Here Reagan lists what he sees as the foreign policy disasters of the Carter government: the Soviet occupation of Afghanistan and the threat to oil supplies; the Soviet Union's superior defence expenditure (no figures are given); the continued imprisonment of the Teheran hostages, now in its eighth month. The only concrete proposal is for an increase in pay for the armed forces.

When we move from domestic affairs and cast our eyes abroad, we see an equally sorry chapter in the record of the present administration . . . . Adversaries large and small test our will and seek to confound our resolve, but the Carter administration gives us weakness when we need strength, vacillation when the times demand firmness.

These are the objectives we seek; first and foremost is the establishment of lasting world peace . . . . But let our friends and those who may wish us ill take note: the United States has an obligation to its citizens and to the people of the world never to let those who would destroy freedom dictate the future course of human life on this planet. I would regard my election as proof that we have renewed our resolve to preserve world freedom and peace. This nation will once again be strong enough to do that.

Source B

Sources B, C and D are from letters sent to *Time* in October and November 1980.

Ronald Reagan will get my vote because he has a positive view of the US . . . . Reagan is for making our country strong and building it even stronger economically, militarily, morally.

Source C

May the Republicans have a landslide victory over the Democrats who are responsible for America's decline from power and restore America to greatness again. For me this convention has been inspiring. More power to the Republicans!

Source D

During the debate [a televised debate between Carter and Reagan] I felt as if I were watching the emperor without his clothes. I saw a politician outfitted by his image-makers; yet the nakedness of his ideas was obvious. His economic and social policies will exploit the powerless, invade the most private aspects of our lives and put us at risk of a major war.

1 What does Reagan think has gone wrong with American society and how would he set out to remedy it?

2 To what sort of people and to what emotions is Reagan's speech designed to appeal?

3 Do sources B, C, and D give any indications of how well the Reagan technique worked?

Reaganomics

Reagan's economic package was a mixture of economics and morality. The press dubbed it 'Reaganomics'. Both taxes and public expenditure were cut, taxes being reduced between 1981 and 1984 by 25 per cent. In 1981 and 1982 the welfare system was overhauled, and programmes aiding the unemployed, one-parent families and the low-paid were slashed by over 10 per cent. Federal subsidies to public transport were axed, as were a number of federal 'watchdog' commissions, such as those overseeing the safety of food and drugs and the environment. Affirmative action programmes were run down.

Supporters of Reaganomics argued that in the long run no one would suffer, because the incentive individuals now had to work harder would stimulate the whole economy and the extra wealth created would 'trickle down' to all levels of society. More jobs would be created, giving people the dignity of supporting their families through their own efforts, and so many extra people would be eligible to pay tax that the federal government would easily make up the income lost in tax cuts. In 1981 Reagan boasted that even with tax cuts he could reduce the budget deficit, or even wipe it out altogether.

This policy ran into trouble during its first two years, when a recession pushed up unemployment to 11 per cent and upset the tax calculations. At the same time, defence expenditure rose sharply. The budget deficit of 1982 was the largest in American history, Reagan's popularity slumped and the Democrats made gains in the mid-term elections. Reagan's luck held, however. By 1984 the recession had eased, unemployment dropped to its lowest level since 1970 and tax cuts meant that four-fifths of Americans were

Among the programmes cut were the Food Stamp Programme, Medicaid (help with medical expenses for the poor) and cheap school lunches. Few cuts were made in social security or Medicare (free medical insurance for the over 65s), because these would have mostly affected the elderly, who were an increasing proportion of the electorate.

A similar policy was followed by the Conservative government in Britain where it was nicknamed 'Thatcherism'.

Budget deficit: the difference between the amount the federal government takes in taxes, etc. and the amount it spends.

This was not accidental. Defence spending was a Reagan priority, and he argued that the country could afford it if social spending were pruned enough.

Unemployed steelworkers and their families queuing for free food in Braddock, Pennsylvania, in 1983. Not everyone benefited from the Reagan economic revolution, but enough Americans did to make the President immensely popular.

The number whose cash income fell below the poverty line rose from 29.3 million in 1980 to 35.3 million in 1984, more than one out of every seven Americans, and the highest proportion since Johnson's war on poverty began.

better off than in 1980. In 1984 Reagan ran against a rather colourless Democrat, Walter Mondale, who had been Carter's Vice-President in 1976-80. Mondale argued the cause of that one-fifth of the population whose standard of living had dropped with the axing of welfare schemes and public services. The Republicans won an even more resounding victory than in 1980, drawing their support from the same areas as before.

The moral majority

Evangelical religious groups claiming to represent the 'moral majority' of ordinary Americans put pressure on the administration to pass laws reversing the 'permissive society'. Among the demands made were – the banning of abortion; restrictions on homosexuals; the reintroduction of the death penalty; morning prayers in schools; an undoing of much of the legislation giving women equal status; and the restoration to local communities of the right to censor textbooks, library books and films.

Fundamentalist religious groups had more success at state level. In March 1981 the Arkansas Legislature ruled that schools that taught the theory of evolution must also teach 'creation science', i.e. the version of creation given in the Old Testament. Opponents argued that it was tantamount to imposing a particular religious view on children.

In 1980 Reagan had stood as the champion of the family and old-fashioned moral values, but he was a shrewd enough politician to sense that many Americans, even among the moral majority, were wary of allowing the Government to interfere too much in the private moral lives of individuals. They feared that such interference would foster intolerance and threaten civil liberties, which many believed distinguished their society from 'godless' communism. While paying lip-service to the moral majority, the President made only a half-hearted effort to steer moral legislation through Congress.

The rebirth of patriotism: Reagan and the world

Reagan wanted to introduce a simple, clear-cut morality into American foreign policy. To many Americans this came as a welcome relief after the doubts and humiliations of the 1970s, but Reagan's strategy encountered considerable opposition in Congress, which surfaced in the debates over Nicaragua and El Salvador in 1982 and 1983. In Nicaragua, Reagan had reversed Carter's support for the Sandanista Government and was backing instead a band of anti-Sandanista guerillas – the Contras. In neighbouring El Salvador the repressive Government received American aid against its own rebels, who were supported by the Sandanistas. When President Reagan asked Congress to approve billions of dollars-worth of aid to anti-Communist forces in Central America, a two-year-long argument ensued.

Source A
Extracts from speeches made by President Reagan in 1982.

The Soviet Union is an evil empire . . . the focus of evil in the modern world . . . . When evil is loose in the world, we are enjoined by scripture and the Lord Jesus to oppose it with all our might.

Let us not delude ourselves. The Soviet Union underlies all the unrest that is going on. If they weren't engaged in this game of dominoes, there wouldn't be any hot spots in the world.

Source B
From a speech by Democratic Senator Dodd during the Senate debate on aid to El Salvador, May 1983.

If Central America were not wracked with poverty, there would be no revolution . . . . I have been to that country [El Salvador], and I know about the morticians who travel the streets each morning to collect the bodies of those summarily dispatched the night before by the Salvadoran security forces.

Source C
From a letter to *Time*, 12 April 1982.

As long as we support and engineer oppressive regimes, we will be faced with anti-American, and therefore usually Communist, revolutions in these countries. Instead of winning friends in the world, our actions ensure that we will be hated in future by the new rulers.

???

1 Why, from the evidence in source A, does Reagan believe that events in Central America concern the United States so closely?

2 What alternative explanations for events in Central America are offered in sources B and C?

3 In the light of this argument, what problems might be created for Reagan's foreign policy and in what ways might he try to get round these problems?

In the end, Congress granted some, but not all, of the funds requested by Reagan, and at the same time specifically ruled that the money should go for economic and humanitarian, not for military, purposes.

The world's policeman again? American troops stand guard over three Grenadan prisoners during the American invasion of the island in October 1983.

Critics pointed out that it would not have been so easy to intervene successfully in a larger country and might have led to the United States getting bogged down in another Vietnam.

The original inhabitants of Palestine, which had been annexed by Israel in 1948 and 1967 and who were now living in exile. The United States was a particular object of hatred because of her friendship with Israel.

Elsewhere, America attempted to resume her role as the world's policeman, although Reagan's words were often more belligerent than his actions. In October 1983 American marines invaded Grenada and removed a revolutionary government that had just overthrown the legally elected regime. Although much criticized by the world at large, this seems to have been welcomed by the majority of the 100,000 Grenadans. In 1982 a peace-keeping force was sent to war-torn Lebanon. When, however, the marine barracks in Beirut was bombed in October 1983, killing 60 Americans, Reagan was faced with the choice of sending in more troops or withdrawing. He chose withdrawal. The lessons of Vietnam had not been completely forgotten, even in 1984.

Anti-Americanism continued to erupt in acts of terrorism against Americans abroad, especially at the hands of Palestinian or Iranian groups. Reagan blamed Colonel Gadhafi of Libya for encouraging this terrorism, and on 15 April 1986 American planes bombed Tripoli, causing some civilian casualties. This raid was greeted with great delight by most Americans as evidence that the United States would no longer lie down passively when her interests or her citizens were threatened. The few voices who asked whether the real causes of anti-Americanism might not go deeper than Gadhafi's villainy went mainly unheeded.

Star Wars

Predictably, relations with the Soviet Union were icy during Reagan's first term. National defence spending rose from $160 billion in 1980 to $274 billion in 1984 and the prospect of a major war suddenly seemed closer than it had done for many years. A public debate, more intense than any since the 1950s, began over the probable human and environmental effects of a nuclear holocaust.

On 23 March 1983 Reagan took the United States and the world by surprise when he announced in a television speech that he had discovered the ultimate weapon – the Strategic Defence Initiative, or SDI, which the press nicknamed Star Wars. Space stations would be put into orbit capable of firing lasers that could stop enemy missiles before they entered the earth's atmosphere. Reagan was ecstatic over the potential of these weapons, which were still at the drawing-board stage. Others were more doubtful.

The Soviet Union played her own part in this worsening of relations. In August 1983 a South Korean civilian airliner which had strayed into Soviet airspace was shot down, killing all 269 aboard. This shocked and angered the West.

A book that made a big impact was *The Fate of the Earth* by Jonathan Schell, which first brought the idea of the nuclear winter to public attention.

Source A
From the television speech by President Reagan, 23 March 1983.

I call on the American scientific community to turn their great talents . . . to the cause of mankind and world peace, to give us the means of rendering nuclear weapons impotent and obsolete . . . . Once our scientists have developed an infallible nuclear defence, no longer will our country have to rely on retaliation to protect us from nuclear attack . . . . What if a free people could live secure in the knowledge that their security didn't rest upon the threat of instant retaliation to deter Soviet attack, that we could intercept and destroy strategic missiles before they reached our soil and that of our allies?

Source B
From George Ball, *The War for Star Wars*, in *New York Review of Books*, 11 April 1985. Ball had been a deputy secretary of state and ambassador under Presidents Roosevelt, Truman, Kennedy and Johnson.

Pre-emptive strike: an attack launched by a country that feels it would be attacked itself sooner or later by its enemies. By striking first it gains the advantage of surprise and wipes out any inherent advantage the other side might have in terms of greater manpower or resources.

The abrupt broadcasting of that unexamined project to the nation – and to the world – was, in my view, one of the most irresponsible acts by any head of state in modern times . . . .
Not even lasers and computers are magical, and any Star Wars defence we might someday develop at exhorbitant cost would be a quickly depreciating investment. The Soviets would never sit idly by watching us struggle to build a shield behind which – as they saw it – we might safely launch a first strike . . . . They would do what other nations have done when presented with a comparable threat – commit whatever resources were required to develop defensive weapons of their own . . . . At the same time they would drastically increase the quality and quantity of their offensive weapons so that by the mass use of new technical counter-measures, they would be able to overwhelm our own defensive systems. Moreover, in the quite unlikely event that they should find themselves being outdistanced, one cannot completely reject the thought that they might strike pre-emptively, just as the Japanese chose to attack Pearl Harbour in 1941 because, by 1943, America would have completed its battleship programme and thus gained decisive naval superiority.

??

1 What system of defence would SDI replace, and what benefits does Reagan think it will bring the United States and the world?

2 Ball sees not benefits in SDI but dangers. What are these dangers?

3 Ball accuses Reagan of being 'irresponsible'. What grounds does Ball have for making this accusation and why should Reagan have rushed to announce the project before it had even got off the ground?

Gorbachev became Party Secretary in March 1985.

In 1985 the new Soviet leader, Mikhail Gorbachev, showed signs of wanting better relations with the United States. In November 1985 the two leaders met at Geneva and again at Reykjavik (Iceland) in October 1986. Reagan claimed that his Star Wars blueprint had frightened the Russians into coming

President Reagan and Soviet leader Gorbachev (left) meet across the table at the Reykjavik summit, 1986, with only their interpreters present.

to the conference table. However, at Reykjavik a far-reaching arms reduction agreement was made dependent by the Russians on the abandonment of SDI. This Reagan refused and the talks broke down. Where the truth of the matter lies is not yet clear.

Conclusion

For six years Ronald Reagan enjoyed great popularity, but in November 1986 the image fell apart, when it was revealed that some of Reagan's aides were involved in a secret deal to sell arms to Iran (on whom the United States had persuaded other nations to place an arms embargo) in return for Iranian aid in freeing American hostages in the Lebanon. The profits made from the sale were then used to buy arms for the Nicaraguan Contras, by-passing Congress' restrictions on military aid to Central America.

It wasn't immediately clear whether Reagan himself was involved in this deception or whether his aides had acted behind his back. Either way, the President's image as a strong and honest leader was shattered. Suddenly he appeared as old and bumbling. Overnight his popularity crumbled, the Democrats made large gains in the November 1986 mid-term elections and the press began to refer to the incident as Reagan's 'Irangate' or 'Contragate'. The verdict of the Senate investigating committee, under ex-Senator Tower of Texas, which reported in March 1987 that Reagan was guilty only of incompetence in failing to supervise his subordinates properly, did not help the President's reputation much. For a while he seemed doomed to be a 'lame duck' President, just going through the motions until his time in office was up. The 1988 Presidential election seemed to be the Democrats' for the taking.

But Reagan's legendary luck held. By the autumn of 1987 the Democrats had failed to produce a convincing Presidential candidate, and important developments were taking place on the international stage. Gorbachev put forward new proposals for scrapping short and medium-range nuclear weapons in Europe and Reagan responded favourably. In December the two leaders held another Summit, this time in Washington, and the Intermediate Nuclear Forces Treaty (INF) was signed. Whether Reagan would go down in history as the discredited President of Irangate, or an international statesman who left the world a little safer than he found it, remained to be seen.

A report in the English newspaper, the *Guardian*, on 20 December 1986 from the Indiana hometown of Admiral Poindexter, one of the White House aides involved in the scandal, revealed the extent to which Reagan's credibility had fallen, even in this staunchly Republican area where over 90 per cent of the votes cast in 1984 had been for Reagan.

The Democrat front-runner, Senator Gary Hart, a married man, was forced to drop out when the press revealed that he had spent a night on board his yacht with a glamorous model.

THE USA

YEAR BY YEAR

SINCE 1945

1945   Death of President Roosevelt and his succession by Truman.
Capitulation of Germany.
Potsdam Conference.
Dropping of first atomic bombs on Hiroshima and Nagasaki and surrender of Japan.
GI Bill of Rights.

1946   Kennan telegram.

1947   Truman Doctrine establishes policy of Containment.
Beginning of Marshall Aid.

1948   Berlin Blockade and airlift begin.
Re-election of Truman.

1949   Truman launches Fair Deal.
Soviet Union explodes her first atom bomb.
Berlin airlift ends.
Establishment of NATO and state of West Germany.
China becomes Communist.

1950   Conviction of Alger Hiss and beginning of McCarthy's anti-Communist crusade.
UN intervention in Korea.

1951   Sacking of General MacArthur.

1952   Election of Eisenhower as President.
Dulles become Secretary of State.

1953   Death of Stalin and succession of Khruschev.
End of Korean War.
US explodes her first hydrogen bomb.

1954   Supreme Court ruling against desegregation in education.
Senate vote of censure against McCarthy.
Beginning of US commitment to South Vietnam.

Adoption of Domino theory.

1955   Montgomery bus boycott begins.
Geneva Summit and Open Skies Plan.

1956   Re-election of Eisenhower.
Desegregation of Montgomery buses.
Soviet invasion of Hungary.

1957   Little Rock incident.
Soviet Union launches first Sputnik.

1958   Publication of *The Affluent Society*.

1959   Castro comes to power in Cuba.
Vice-President Nixon visits the Soviet Union and Khruschev visits USA.

1960   U2 incident and failed Paris summit.
SNCC-sponsored sit-ins begin.
Election of President Kennedy.

1961   Peace Corps founded.
Freedom Rides begin.
Gagarin becomes first man in space and Kennedy launches Moon Programme.
Bay of Pigs invasion.

1962   John Glenn becomes the first American to orbit earth.
Cuban Missile Crisis.

1963   Great civil rights demonstration in Washington.
Hot line and partial Test Ban Treaty.
First US marines go to Vietnam.
Assassination of Kennedy.

1964   Johnson launches Great Society.
Civil Rights Bill passed.
Freedom Summer in Mississippi.
First student protests at Berkeley, California.
Re-election of Johnson.
Gulf of Tonkin resolution.

Downfall of Khruschev and his replacement by Brezhnev.

1965   Voting Rights Act.
Watts riots.

1967   Counter-culture reaches its height with the 'Summer of peace and love'.

1968   Student disturbances reach their height.
Riots at Democratic Party Chicago convention.
Assassinations of Robert Kennedy and Martin Luther King.
Johnson decides not to stand for re-election.
Election of Nixon.
Tet offensive.

1969   Moon landing.
Trial of Chicago Eight

1970   US invasion of Cambodia and killing of students at Kent State, Ohio, by National Guard.

1971   Publication of Pentagon Papers.
US table-tennis team invited to China.

1972   ERA passed by Congress.
Watergate break-in.
Re-election of Nixon. Nixon's visits to Soviet Union and China mark height of Detente.
SALT I signed.

1973   Watergate conspiracy begins to unravel.
Removal of Vice-President Agnew and his replacement with Gerald Ford.
Incident at Wounded Knee, South Dakota.
Yom Kippur War and oil crisis.
Ceasefire and withdrawal of US ground troops from Vietnam.
Overthrow of Allende in Chile.

1974 Resignation of Nixon.
Ford becomes President.

1975 Near-bankruptcy of New York City.
Church Committee reveal illegal acts by past Presidents.
Fall of South Vietnam and Cambodia to Communists.

1976 Election of President Carter.
Bicentennial year

1977 Launching of Carter's unsuccessful energy-saving plan.

1978 Camp David Accords.

1979 Fall of Shah of Iran and seizure of US hostages.

Sandanistas seize power in Nicaragua.
Soviet invasion of Afghanistan and Carter's retaliatory measures.

1980 Inflation reaches 13.5 per cent and unemployment 8.5 million.
Election of President Reagan.

1981 Release of the Teheran hostages.

1982 Record budget deficit.
US peace-keeping force sent to Lebanon.

1983 Congress limits aid to Central America.
Invasion of Grenada.
Bombing of US marine barracks in Beirut.

Reagan announces Star Wars project.

1984 Unemployment falls to under 6 per cent.
Re-election of Reagan.
Withdrawal from Lebanon.

1985 Mikhail Gorbachev becomes Soviet leader.
Geneva Summit between Reagan and Gorbachev.

1986 Irangate scandal bursts.
Reykjavik Summit.
Bombing of Tripoli by US airforce.

1987 Gary Hart drops out as Democratic presidential candidate for 1988.
Washington Summit.
INF Treaty signed.

BOOK LIST

Histories of the USA:
P. Hill *A History of the USA*, 1974
P. Nash and J. Jeffery ed., *The American People vol.2*, 1986
G. Hodgson, *America in our Time*, 1977

Books that cover particular aspects of post-1945 US history:
C. Bernstein and R. Woodward, All the Presidents Men, 1974 – Watergate *The Final Days*, 1975 – Watergate
B.J. Bersnstein, *The Atomic Bomb*, 1976
M. Charlton and A. Moncrieff, *Many Reasons Why: The American Involvement in Vietnam*, 1978 – in conjunction with the BBC
Alistair Cooke, *Talking about America 1951-1968*, 1981
F. Graham Jr, *Since Silent Spring*, 1970 – the ecology issue
T. Hayden, *True*, 1971 – story of the Chicago 8
R. Kennedy, *Thirteen Days. The Cuban Missile Crisis October 1962*, 1969
W. Manchester, *Death of a President*, 1967 – the assassination of President Kennedy
J. McGinnis, *The Selling of the President*

1968, 1970
C. Mee Jr, *Meeting at Potsdam*, 1975 – the origins of the Cold War
W. O'Neil, *Coming Apart. An Unofficial History of the 1960s*, 1971
B. Quarles, *The Negro in the Making of America*, 1969 – the last three chapters
M. Voise, *Fire in the Streets*, the youth rebellion of the 1960s
T. Wolfe, *The Right Stuff*, 1979 – the story of the first astronauts

Biographies and Autobiographies:
Eldridge Cleaver, *Soul on Ice*, 1967 – one black American's experience
E.F. Goldman, *The Tragedy of Lyndon Johnson*, 1969
Alex Haley (ed.), *The Autobiography of Malcolm X*, 1965
D. Lewis, *Martin Luther King, a critical biography*, 1970
R.M. Nixon, *The Memoirs of Richard Nixon*, 1978
D. Parks, *G.I. Diary*, 1968 – a Vietnam experience
A. Schlessinger, *Robert Kennedy and his Times*, 1978

P. Salinger, *With Kennedy*, 1966

Anthologies:
Alistair Cooke, *The Americans, Letters from America 1969-1979*
A. Nevin, *The Burden and the Glory*, 1964 – the speeches of President Kennnedy
J.P. Colin and C.H. Peterson *An American Harvest*, 1986 – key documents

Books that made an impact on America in this period:
J. Baldwin, *The Fire next Time*, 1963 – foretold the black rebellion of the 1960s
D. Brown, *Bury my Heart at Wounded Knee*, 1971
B. Frieden, *The Feminine Mystique*, 1963 – the first Feminist book
J.K. Galbraith, *The Affluent Society*, 1958
Martin Luther King, *Why We can't Wait*, 1964
R. Morgan ed., *Sisterhood is Powerful*, 1970 – published at the height of the Feminist revolt
C. Reich, *The Greening of America*, 1970

BIOGRAPHICAL
NOTES

Agnew, Spiro T. (1918-)
Republican Vice-President of the US 1968-73. Resigned over tax-evasion charges.

Armstrong, Neil (1930-) First man to walk on the moon, 1969.

Brezhnev, Leonid I. (1906-82) First Secretary of the Communist Party of the Soviet Union and effective Soviet leader from 1964 to his death in 1982.

Carmichael, Stokeley (1942-) SNCC leader in the early 1960s and one of the first spokesmen for Black Power.

Carter, James E., 'Jimmy' (1924-) Democrat Governor of Georgia 1970-4; President of the USA 1976-80.

Castro, Fidel (1926-) Left-wing guerilla leader who seized power in Cuba in 1959 and has held it ever since. Feared and distrusted by the US.

Church, Frank (1924-) Democrat Senator for Idaho.

Diem, Ngo Dinh (1901-63) Anti-Communist, American-backed President of South Vietnam 1955-63. Overthrown and assassinated by a military coup in 1963.

Dulles, John Foster (1888-1959) US Secretary of State for Foreign Affairs 1953-9. Author of the doctrines of 'roll back' and 'massive nuclear retaliation'.

Eisenhower, Dwight D., 'Ike' (1890-1969). Republican. Supreme Allied Commander in Europe 1943-5 and Supreme Commander NATO 1950-2. President of US 1952-60.

Ellsberg, Daniel (1931-) State Department official 1964-70. Closely involved in the running of the Vietnam War. Turned against the war in the late 1960s. Leaked Pentagon Papers to *The New York Times* in 1971.

Ervin, Sam, (1897-1985) Democrat. Senator for North Carolina. Regarded as Senate's leading authority on constitutional law and therefore chosen to be Chairman of Senate Committee set up to investigate the Watergate break-in 1973-4.

Ford, Gerald R. (1913-) Republican. Congressman for Michigan 1948-73. Vice-President 1973-4, President of USA 1974-6.

Gadhafi, Colonel Muammer (1942-) Ruler of Libya since a military coup that overthrew the King in 1969. Devout Muslim and outspoken enemy of the US.

Gorbachev, Mikhail S. (1931-) First Secretary of the Communist Party since March 1985. Youngest post-war Soviet leader and instigator of a more open society – *Glasnost*.

Harriman, Averell (1891-1986) Democrat. Ambassador to Soviet Union 1943-6 and member of the Truman and Johnson administrations. Chief negotiator of 1963 Test Ban Treaty and US representative at abortive peace talks with North Vietnam in 1968. Proponent of Detente.

Hayden, Tom (1941-) Founder member of the New Left SDS in 1962 and student activist of 1960s. One of the Chicago Eight. Now a state Senator for California and married to actress Jane Fonda.

Humphrey, Hubert H. (1911-78) Democrat. Liberal Senator for Minnesota 1948-64. As leader of Democrats in the Senate 1961-4, he played a large part in guiding through the Test Ban Treaty and Civil Rights Bill. Vice-President 1964-8 and supporter of Johnson line in Vietnam. Democratic candidate 1968, defeated by Nixon.

Hiss, Alger (1904-) Former US State Department official who was convicted of perjury in 1950 for denying before a Senate Committee that he had passed secret documents to a Soviet agent in the 1930s.

Johnson, Lyndon Baines (1908-73) Democrat. Democratic leader in the Senate 1955-60. Vice-President 1960-3 and President 1963-8. Responsible for 1964 Civil Rights Bill and Great Society anti-poverty programme; also for escalation of US involvement in Vietnam after Gulf of Tonkin resolution. Decided not to seek re-election in 1968.

Kennan, George (1904-) Career diplomat and author (on political and historical themes) whose telegram from Moscow in 1946 was influential in creating policy of Containment. US ambassador to Soviet Union 1952-3.

Kennedy, John F. (1917-63)
Senator for Massachusetts 1952-60 and President of USA 1960-3. A cautious liberal and Cold War warrior, who was also an exponent of Detente (although it wasn't called that in his day), whose post-mortem reputation is probably over-inflated. Assassinated in Dallas, Texas, 22 November 1963.

Kennedy, Robert (1925-68)
Democrat and brother of John Kennedy. A lawyer, he became his brother's Attorney-General in 1961. Member of Cuban Missile Crisis team. Probable Democratic candidate in 1968 and convert against the Vietnam War, he was shot in Los Angeles in 1968.

Khomeini, Ayatolleh Ruhdlah (1900-) Iranian Islamic religious leader, who spent the years 1964-79 in exile for his opposition to the Shah. Returned in 1979 to head new Islamic government that succeeded the Shah.

Khruschev, Nikita S. (1894-1971)
First Secretary of Soviet Communist Party 1953-64 and Prime Minister 1958-64. Broke the mold of absolute hostility towards the West that had been Stalin's hallmark after 1945 and made possible the thaws of 1959-60 and 1963-4. Responsible for putting the missiles on Cuba that provoked the Cuban Missile Crisis in 1962. Removed from power by the Politburo in 1964 and died quietly in retirement.

King, Martin Luther Jr (1929-68)
Baptist minister and civil rights leader. President of Southern Christian Leadership Conference (SCLC) and advocate of non-violence. Assassinated by a white man, James Earl Ray, in Memphis, Tennessee, in 1968.

MacArthur, General Douglas (1880-1964) US military commander in the Pacific 1942-5 and military governor of occupied Japan. Commander of UN forces in Korea 1950-1. Sacked by Truman for publicly disagreeing with the President's policy.

Marshall, General George (1880-1959) Army Chief of Staff 1939-45. Attempted – in vain – to settle the differences between the Communists and Nationalists in China in 1945-6. Secretary of State 1945-50 and architect of the Marshall Plan to rebuild the economies of Europe.

McCarthy, Joseph (1907-57)
Republican. Senator for Wisconsin 1946-57. His accusation in 1950 that the State Department was harbouring secret Communists began the intense anti-Communist crusade of the early 1950s known as McCarthyism. His influence waned when the Senate passed a vote of censure against him in December 1954.

McGovern, George (1923-)
Democratic and liberal Senator for South Dakota 1962-80. Democratic Presidential candidate 1972.

McNamara, Robert (1916-)
Secretary of Defence under Kennedy and Johnson 1961-7. A supporter of US involvement in Vietnam who later became a 'dove'. Resigned in 1967 and became President of the World Bank.

Meredith, James (1943-) First Black to enter the all-white Mississippi State University at Oxford, Miss., in 1962.

Mondale, Walter (1928-)
Democrat. Liberal Senator for Minnesota 1964-76. Vice-President 1976-80. Unsuccessful Presidential candidate 1984.

Nixon, Richard M. (1913-)
Republican. Senator for California 1950-2, member of Committee on Un-American Activities during McCarthy era and prosecutor of Alger Hiss. Vice-President 1952-60. Defeated Republican presidential candidate 1960. President 1968-74. Withdrew US from Vietnam 1974 and began normalization of relations with China. Forced to resign over Watergate scandal 1974.

Oswald, Lee Harvey (1939-63) Ex-marine, who had defected to the Soviet Union in 1959 and back again in 1962. Arrested 22 November 1963 for the murder of President Kennedy but was himself killed by night-club owner, Jack Ruby, before he could be brought to trial.

Reagan, Ronald (1911-)
Republican. Movie actor who became Governor of California 1966-74. Elected as President 1980 and again in 1984.

Roosevelt, Franklin D. (1882-1945) Democrat, who was first elected as President in 1932. Architect of New Deal. Re-elected a record number of times – 1936, 1940 and 1944. Led US through the Second World War and died at beginning of fourth term of office, April 1945.

Somoza, General Anastasio (1926-) President of Nicaragua 1967-79. The third successive member of his family to rule Nicaragua as a dictator. Supported by the US as a bulwark against communism in the area. Removed in a left-wing revolution by the Sandanistas in 1979 and died in exile in US.

Shah of Iran, Mohammed Reza Pahlavi (1919-80) Autocratic ruler of Iran since 1941. Restored to throne with US backing after being ousted in a constitutional row with Prime Minister Mossadegh in 1953. Ally of US until his overthrow in a popular revolution in January 1979 which brought an anti-American Islamic regime under the Ayatollah Khomeini to power. Died in exile.

Stalin, Joseph V. (1879-1953) First Secretary of the Communist Party of the Soviet Union 1922-53 and dictator 1929-1953. Led the Soviet Union through the Second World War and rebuilt her economy after. Deeply suspicious of the West. Architect of the bloc of Soviet satellites in Eastern Europe known as the 'Iron Curtain'.

Truman, Harry S. (1884-1972)
Democrat. Senator for Missouri 1934-44. Vice-President 1944-5, becoming President after death of Roosevelt. Re-elected in 1948. Architect of the Truman Doctrine. Did not run for re-election in 1952 but remained influential inside the Democrat Party.

INDEX

The figures in **bold type** refer to the pages on which illustrations appear